· R. Varzuga

· Bhutan

Lake
urkana
Lake ·   · Kiwayu
undu   · Malindi
      · Mnemba, Zanzibar

Bora Bora·

Lake Taupo
            ·R. Waikato
·Lake Rotoroa·

Cancer and Pisces

Dana,

With affection and gratitude

Mick

2.x.20

Mick May

Cancer and Pisces

One man's story of his unique
survival of cancer, interwoven with
the joy and succour of fishing

Quiller

Copyright © 2020 Mick May

First published in the UK in 2020
by Quiller, an imprint of Quiller Publishing Ltd

British Library Cataloguing-in-Publication Data
A catalogue record for this book is available
from the British Library

ISBN 978-1-84689-333-9

The right of Mick May to be identified as
the author of this work has been asserted
in accordance with the Copyright, Design
and Patent Act 1988

Design by Guy Callaby

Photographs and other archive materials
are the copyright/property of the author
unless otherwise stated and credited

Printed in Malta

Quiller
An imprint of Quiller Publishing Ltd

Wykey House, Wykey,
Shrewsbury SY4 1JA
Tel: 01939 261616
Email: info@quillerbooks.com
Website: www.quillerpublishing.com

Contents

Foreword

I have never caught a fish in my life but I am hooked on this tale. Mick May's inspirational story darts, leaps and surprises in a trajectory as exciting as that of any brown trout or Atlantic salmon in a fighting mood. His concise chapters often leave the reader gasping, sometimes with laughter, occasionally in tears and constantly with admiration for this book's hero and author.

I have a small walk on part in this story akin to that of an assistant ghillie. Right at the start of Mick's terminal mesothelioma diagnosis in 2013 he called me in an elaborate off-hand way to ask: 'Are you doing anything this afternoon, Jonathan?' I sensed something was wrong. Half an hour later I was at his bedside in the Cromwell Hospital. On my arrival Mick said: 'I asked you to come because you are my only friend who knows the first thing about God'. So we talked. At the end of my visit I said: 'I'd like to do for you what some friends did for me when I was in deep trouble. I will come and see you once a week from now on.'

Our regular meetings were not pious encounters. As always with Mick there were laughs, stories, jokes, eccentricities, anecdotes and many fishermen's tales. Yet the dark cloud of medical realism always lurked in the background. Mesothelioma is invariably a fatal cancer, which usually kills swiftly at best within a year or two. My assignment as Mick's confessor seemed destined to be a brief one.

But it was not. In his ordinary routines as in his cancer struggles, Mick is a life-enhancing optimist whose resilience derives from an inner core of steely courage. So he fought harder and hung on longer than anyone expected. At one point in these pages I am quoted as saying to Mick just as he was about to undergo chemotherapy for the first time: 'I hope you are going to be steady on parade'.

This crass drill sergeant's exhortation is described by Mick as 'the finest non-medical advice I received in all the times of my illness'. Generous, but wrong.

In fact, the prize for sustaining Mick goes not to any of his advisers - practical, spiritual, familial or even medical. I suspect to understand this the reader needs to enter Mick's beloved hinterland – his mystical world of Pisces.

The characters in and around Mick's Piscean universe are worthy of a Balzac novel. They start with the author's eccentric father, 'Crackers' May DSO OBE MC, and his similarly individual mother, Liz. On his beloved River Test, Mick introduces his exuberant Tigger-like surgeon, Professor Loic Lang-Lazdunski, to his first ever day of fishing. The mayflies are hatching, Loic swiftly catches three fine trout and is so enraptured that he has now become 'a regular on the river'.

This book sees many fishing expeditions and to a range of destinations. You will, for example, travel often with Mick to Scotland and indeed much further afield to Iceland, Argentina and Russia. There, on the Varzuga River, the local guide, unable to master even the simplest English, bestows on Mick a supremely appropriate title in Russian: 'The one who is always happy'.

On any fishing day, indeed almost at any time, Mick is always happy. His *joie de vivre*, his contented family life, his laughter and the love of friends are surely part of the explanation why this 'compleat' and contented angler has survived, indeed thrived, during his mesothelioma struggle of more than seven years.

But the clouds hang always in the background. Throughout the story the ecstasy of the riverbank is counterbalanced by the agony of the hospital room.

Despite round after round of chemo and being a guinea pig on new treatment trials in hospitals from

Lille to Leicester, the killer tumour in Mick's lung is ever-present and the challenge is to stay one step ahead of it for as long as possible. This he has done with astonishing and ground-breaking success thanks to his own courage and with his doctors' revolutionary treatments, which may yet have far-reaching implications for many other mesothelioma victims.

What a story! And to my mind it would have been impossible had not Mick's *Pisces* met his *Cancer*. This is an extraordinary book, a fisherman's tale with a difference about the hero who got away to laugh cheerfully and live on against all the odds.

This well-written tale of humanity and humour in the face of a daunting prognosis combines so much entertainment, encouragement and inspiration that it deserves to be a bestseller.

Jonathan Aitken
29 April 2020

My world changes: 20 May 2013

'Mick, might you go and see a chest specialist in London this afternoon?'

'Medic, it's Friday and I'm looking forward to a quiet weekend in the country. Do I really have to flog into London?'

'Yes, you do, and I've booked an appointment with Brian O'Connor at 3pm.'

I had been driving around the M25 when I took this call from my dear old friend (and GP) Simon 'Medic' Moore. I had seen him three days prior having felt a little out of breath and, as a precaution, he had prevailed on me to have an X-ray. My immediate reaction was to surmise what a worrier my doctor is.

Brian turned out to be an amusing and likeable Irishman with cramped quarters in Pennant Mews behind the Cromwell Hospital. I sat in his waiting room with two or three other unfortunates, bored out of my mind. Eventually I was ushered into a consulting room in which you couldn't swing a cat.

He showed me a picture – the X-ray from the previous day. I remember the rib cage being clearly visible. The bottom right hand side of the picture was just a hazy cloud. I cast my mind back to a medical in late 2010 when another X-ray had shown up a small shadow in a not wholly different spot.

'Ah,' I said, 'the relic of a bout of pleurisy in the early nineties'.

'Not so sure', he replied. 'I'd like you to come into hospital tonight so we can have a look at you'.

'Desperately sorry, but I've got to pick up Daisy, my ten year old, in an hour or so; my wife's away at the moment and I've a quiet and relaxing weekend planned.'

'Well, Monday then.' Brian persists.

'Desperately sorry again; I'm off fishing.'

At that point, he and Medic consulted by telephone, apparently over what an unreasonable patient I was being, but something, somehow, advised them that fishing should win out, so the tests were set for Tuesday. Off I set for my weekend, aware that a cloud might have arrived on the horizon, but nothing more than that.

Monday 20 May saw hardly a break in a resolutely overcast sky – a real match for my mood. Over the weekend I had pondered a little more on what Brian had said and I didn't like the sound of it.

Four brown trout on the bank diverted my ruminations for a while. Nonetheless, the nagging but unascertainable doubts were never that far absent.

The beast and the beauty: late May and early June 2013

Mesothelioma – a word I had never previously heard of. And, as my notes of that year will bear witness, one whose spelling alone defeated me for roughly a month or so. But a word I was to hear increasingly, especially when prefaced with another – 'malignant'.

So here's a quick and necessarily black-and-white explanation of what this beast is, namely a particularly vicious form of cancer. It is invariably fatal and the median life expectancy from diagnosis is around ten months. It is the only form of cancer solely caused by exposure to asbestos, most usually in the workplace. The disease principally affects the pleura (the external lining of the lung) and less often the peritoneum (the lining of the digestive tract). Many cases are diagnosed at an advanced stage as symptoms (for example, breathing trouble and unexplained chest pains), are typically non-specific and appear late in the development of the disease. Sufferers tend to die a painful death, lungs constricted by an ever-hardening lining.

It turns out that the UK has the highest incidence of mesothelioma per head of population in the world. It claims 2,500 deaths a year of which eighty-four per cent are men and sixteen per cent women – a reflection of more traditional working patterns in the heavy industrial and construction sectors of three or four decades ago; the average period between exposure to asbestos and the manifestation of the disease is between twenty-five and forty years.

The progression from some hope to none (apparently) was swift. On 21 May I went to the Cromwell for a procedure known as 'drainage' to remove what everyone presumed from the X-ray was liquid on the lung. From the amount and analysis of it the experts would have a good idea of what was troubling me. Things can often move glacially in hospitals and so it was that about four hours after arrival and under local anaesthetic a doctor shoved a tube into my back and plugged the other end into a bag. All very peaceful to begin with until at some point I sat up in bed and everything changed. What had been a trickle transmogrified itself into a torrent, filling successive 600ml bags with rapidity. In all, nearly five of them; just about three litres of the stuff. Another way to think of it is that I went home three kilos lighter, having lost four per cent of my body weight in about thirty minutes. This was accompanied by a concern, which was more than nagging, that everyone had been expecting a lot less fluid.

Just before I left the hospital, Brian O'Connor referred to some 'irregularities' in samples he had just looked at. The following day he called me again and firmly asked me to come to London immediately. I drove up in something of a lather; good news surely would have been given to me over the telephone. As soon as I was shown into his room he suggested we ask my wife, Jill, to join us, saying something like: 'It's often better on this sort of occasion'. Good Lord! This must really be serious, I thought.

Jill beetled over from her new assignment at the Competition and Markets Authority, looking the epitome of professional competence. There was no beating about the bush from Brian. The recommendation was a biopsy, and then a question: had I ever been exposed to asbestos at an early stage? In my stupefaction, all I could recall was a single chemistry lesson at my prep school when the teacher held a piece of asbestos over a Bunsen burner. Unlikely to cause any harm, he thought. Had we ever heard of mesothelioma? Neither of us had; then he explained it was a form of cancer directly linked to that material. This was done with great gentleness, but the brutality of the probable diagnosis was there right before us. That this was a lung cancer we had each separately deduced, and, from the little we then knew, an unpleasant one. And, with another indicator of the gravity of where we were, he pleaded with us not to check it out on the internet. First, we had to establish whether his worst fears were correct and, secondly, there was every chance that the prognosis for me was likely to be better than the statistics quoted there. Each sentence of his felt like a blow to my stomach. I looked across at Jill. She was weeping quietly.

What next? Well, he would book the biopsy for that Friday. Oh, and by chance the surgeon, Professor Loic Lang-Lazdunski, was across the road in the Cromwell right then. My initial reaction, mercifully unspoken, was that if this was what meeting doctors brought you, I wasn't sure I could face another.

And so, in the early evening, we sat down with Loic for the first time. I'm not sure exactly what I was expecting a surgeon so eminent, ground-breaking even, to be like. I was certainly prepared to encounter high levels of confidence, possibly bordering on arrogance. And, in my understandably frail emotional state, I anticipated having to face further devastating truths, most probably insensitively delivered.

Into a smallish consulting room walked an early middle-aged man; the first thing I noticed was a beaming smile. Next his low-key manner became apparent – the very opposite of what I was expecting, coupled with a clear sympathy with his patients. My spirits picked up, and, looking across the desk, I had a sure premonition that he was going to play a pivotal role in the remainder of my life. Indeed, indeed ...

The next ten days or so seemed to pass in something of a blur. Each morning I would wake up certain I had just had a nightmare and for a blissful five minutes my normal life opened up before me. And then with a dull thump my new and real world returned.

I had my biopsy and sure enough I had mesothelioma – by this stage it would have been unthinkable that I didn't. But it was 'epithelioid', advised Loic, the best type to treat. Plus I was young, and fit, and so on and so forth. His optimism appeared boundless, which, fed to one of nature's Tiggers, created in my mind a condition akin to pulmonary diabetes.

And my condition was operable. I was going to have something called a 'radical pleurectomy and decortication'. In layman's terms, Loic was going to scrape all the cancer off the pleura, the gap between my lungs and my ribcage. This radically altered things, I was advised. First, it would offer me remission; there would literally be no cancer in my body for a time. It would come back though, that much I knew. However, the statistics were impressive. Sixty per cent of his patients lived for three years or more and forty per cent for five years plus. I'm having that, I thought.

The operation was scheduled for 12 June and, as the prospect of it loomed ever closer, I tried to view it as most of my recent male relatives must have anticipated military action. And so I called it 'my own personal Capuzzo'. I have always preferred not to think of my cancer as a battle, even then. The notion gives hope to a vast multitude, I know, and certainly it is better to show bravery than to become a gibbering wreck. My view is, however, that we sufferers just have to get on with our lives as best we can. So it is, in truth, self-preservation.

So why Capuzzo? This is a fort in North Africa, near the Libyan-Egyptian border, which played a significant role in the Western Desert campaign of the Second World War. It is where my father won his Military Cross in 1941, leading his men from the Durham Light Infantry in a heroic charge. At his funeral, one of his former soldiers spoke to me glowingly of the courage and sangfroid Dad had displayed that day; looking back on that conversation I decided that it was these virtues to which I aspired.

This did not mean that I was always calm in this period. Anything but. I tried to be upbeat. But from time to time my emotions boiled over in anger and frustration at how this could be happening.

And in the midst of all of this and as if in a form of recompense, came 2 June, a day of almost indescribable peace and beauty on the River Dun, just above where it flows into the larger River Test. The weather was near-perfect, a warm sunny day with the odd bit of cloud cover. The buttercups were in full bloom and the birds were singing loudly. And that best of omens, a kingfisher darting upstream in a flash of deep turquoise as we lugged our lunch and other gear to the picnic table. It was 11.30 and already the mayfly hatch had begun, tentatively at first, but we knew it would pick up during the day.

As he was there on this epic day, it is time to introduce Graham Wood. Angling is predominantly a solitary activity. You fish on your own and one of its primary joys is the solitude and peace. However, a day spent with someone else is always richer, not least because the easy pace of life is a sure route to understanding people better. In consequence, I have always taken greater pleasure in sharing my days on the riverbank. I have at least a dozen good mates who share my passion; but I also love seeing others, and especially members of my family, get the bug. To do that you need to ensure that your guest will actually catch something. So from the early days of my time on the Test I have taken a ghillie along to coach others (and me too, more often than I care to admit).

About a dozen years ago I was introduced to Graham. Over time we have struck up a sincere friendship. He is highly knowledgeable about birdlife, insects and of course trout. He is also a natural teacher, combining technical skill with ability to explain and impart it. And as a bonus he is patient and a true 'people person' with a wicked sense of humour. As a result he crops up frequently in this story, not least because any expedition in his company is always going to be more fun.

On this memorable day, my guest Dulce and I set off in differing directions, she upstream with Graham Wood to guide her, and I downstream into the shady wooded part of the beat. Within a very short while I was in another world, mentally further from the Cromwell Hospital than I was geographically. Swiftly I was to be rewarded for my strategy of casting to the opposite bank underneath overhanging branches, one which comes with great risk of many lost flies. Nothing ventured ... I spotted a biggish shape in the water and cast to it with a Mayfly Emerger. This it inspected but wouldn't take. So I switched to another Mayfly and bingo! A four-and-three-quarter-pound brown trout landed some minutes later. Perfect.

At lunchtime we were joined by Jill and our daughter, India-Rose. A happy conversation ensued, mainly on diet. Dulce had beaten breast cancer, taking to heart what she ate and ascribing her survival in part to it. Graham nodded and tucked into a pork pie.

Then it was on with the fishing. India volunteered to give it a go, and was rewarded with a two-and-a-half pounder followed by another a little later. Jill then had a shot, and in spite of what Graham described as a 'fine but muscular style' struck lucky too. So, by 4.30–5.00pm the tally was eight and I found myself a little surprised that Jill hadn't forcibly rested me in the deckchair we had brought along for the purpose. I suspected she had been too busy arranging my life. During the afternoon, Loic's office confirmed that the big operation was set for the following week. With a sinking heart, I hastened back to the river lest I became depressed.

By early evening Graham and I were alone and fishing the upstream (sunny) side of the Dun, where the hatch was the best he had seen all season, he said. Two more on the bank, then a rest and back down to the glade. By this point I was pooped and making lots of silly mistakes, something of which Graham was more than aware, though he was way too gentlemanly to comment. His only aim appeared to be to get me off the river by 8.00pm, the time he had promised Jill. I had little intention of departing a moment before. The pool below the bridge by the picnic table had always enticed me, though I had never previously been successful. I saw two rises, and put a fly over one then the other. Further joy!

At about 7.45 we filled in the fishing book in the hut. Technically – that is, according to the club rules – I had hit my limit of seven fish, but the girls, combined, had caught only four. My reasoning was, therefore, that 'we' were three short of their seven. On the basis that the club secretary will never read this memoir or, should that happen, understands the context within which I bent the rules a smidgeon, we headed up the river at 7.00pm. By 8.15 I had hooked and released just that number.

Every so often a violent storm intrudes on a beautiful sunny day. When it does, the brightness of the landscape in the near and middle distance is enhanced by the cobalt blue of the threatening sky. In a similar manner, the joy of this near-immaculate afternoon and evening was only heightened by the impending medical tempest.

Why?

Why on earth would anyone write a recollection linking one's suffering, in my case cancer, and fly-fishing?

It was something I had never considered until at some point author and former politician Jonathan Aitken, whom I know well, suggested it to me as a project. Immediately I dismissed it as patently ridiculous. One brings to my mind sunlit hours on some glorious riverbank; the other tends to summon up images of misery. Surely they are completely unsuited bedfellows?

And yet, and yet ... as time progressed the idea started to become increasingly less daft, until I realised on Easter Day 2019 – on, strangely, a paddleboard in Salcombe Harbour – that it made perfect sense.

First, because as I have moved through the chapters of my illness one way or another a day's fishing, or the prospect of one, has never been too far distant, and mercifully often very close indeed. And time spent angling in a variety of settings has always raised my spirits when they needed lifting, thanked those who needed thanking and provided the perfect impetus for withstanding the rigours of treatment.

Secondly, this passion of mine happens to be the UK's biggest participant sport, enjoyed by hundreds of thousands of souls, and millions worldwide. Statistics being what they are, therefore, it is a sad likelihood that tens of thousands of lovers of the sport in this country alone will be afflicted by tumours each and every year. Curiously, though, there would appear to be no specific works linking them.

Finally, of course, fishing may be viewed just as a metaphor. I have recorded some of the thrills and triumphs I have enjoyed from the riverbank, but for others these might be replaced by their different passions. It is merely a case of what ignites the individual.

And as I have written this very personal (and probably ridiculously idiosyncratic) memoir I have greatly enjoyed the process. It has been made fun, and from time to time very painful, because I have been able to move between four sets of records – what the mediaeval historian in me might call 'sources'.

Those who have any idea of the nonchalance with which I view all sorts of filing or the balancing of my current account (piles of paper mount up on my desk and bank statements remain routinely unopened) would be taken aback by the near-Prussian standards of discipline I apply to a few aspects of my life. For example,

I have kept an up-to-date fishing book since August 1986. In this, now spanning two volumes and the first of my sources, I record each day spent fishing – the location, the weather, the catch, who accompanied me, and the flies or lures used. This has enabled me to pinpoint the actual detail on days otherwise incompletely remembered or indeed wholly forgotten.

The second is a diary written between May 2013 and Christmas of that year – very much my annus horribilis. It has an entry for every day and chronicles (a rather grand word) what happened to me, and how I felt about it. This covers, then, the moment of my diagnosis – or, rather, moments, plural, since realisation seems to arrive in a slow-motion cascade rather than a bombshell – to the end of my first 'line' (series of six treatments) of chemotherapy. As you might imagine it is in places an emotionally stark record, full of shock, but even here there is the odd attempt at humour.

Next, I have always found pleasure in taking photographs. I bought my first semi-pro camera, a Pentax K1000 which I still have, on my twenty-first birthday, and have kept every negative from that and its successors; they live in several boxes in the attic. In the pre-digital era, like so many others, I stuck the best of the accompanying prints in leather-bound albums. I nearly succumbed to the temptation that befell so many of my contemporaries of switching from this archaic and now expensive way of preserving photos, but the enthusiasm of my children (who love looking at pictures of their younger selves) and the time afforded me in my fortnightly trips to Lille between July 2016 and October 2017 got me up to date. In our bookshelves are thirty-five albums. And, of course, I have thousands of digital images on my PC.

Finally, over the past six or more years a record is produced each time I have a consultation with this or that specialist. So I have copious letters (in English and for a fifteen-month period in French) chronicling my medical progress, or lack of it.

With these, then, as the paints on the palette, I have been able to move from one to the other to recreate this or that representation of a chapter of my life.

My formative years: 1958–1986

You would have thought, wouldn't you, that growing up in rural Northumberland would have given me all the opportunity I needed to become an adept angler at a very young age? But it didn't happen that way.

Nowadays the Tyne is a destination for enthusiasts seeking a reliable source of salmon. Sadly, in the 1960s and '70s the pollution at its mouth had yet to be cleaned up and though there were trout to be found they definitely weren't easy. Add to this the facts that my father didn't fish, we lived all of a dozen miles from the North Tyne and I couldn't drive until I was eighteen and you quickly grasp that catching anything on my own was a heady task.

But something was buried in my psyche, clearly. Three miles from us were some reservoirs. I knew them well because, in those less health-and-safety-conscious days, I would be dropped off at them to walk home if I had misbehaved on the car journey back from school – a routine occurrence. Armed with a metal rod and the most basic of reels (the two costing all of a fiver and using up the entirety of my savings) I went there aged ten and caught my first fish; it probably weighed half a pound. But I can still recall the adrenalin and the weather and everything. And I remember my mother's shock when I announced I wanted to sleep with it.

I often say that I've only ever done two clever things in my life.

The first of these was to be born to my parents, the second taking place some thirty years later. When you reach your teens I think it's normal to think of your parents as the height of embarrassment, and quite probably the most mundane people in the universe. The first was undoubtedly true for me, but the second manifestly not. Though each strived to be conventional it was plain for all to see that Crackers and Liz May were pretty eccentric.

My father had been a career soldier, rising over time to the rank of brigadier and highly decorated to boot.[1] But the impression that most would have taken away from meeting him was of what his obituary in the *Daily Telegraph* accurately recorded as his 'irrepressible sense

---

[1] Though I was slow to recognise it, the fact that my father, grandfather, great uncle and uncle each won the Military Cross is, I think, somewhat unusual. As well as his MC, Crackers was also awarded the DSO and was three times mentioned in despatches.

In 1986 the Imperial War Museum recorded him in a two-hour tape available on its website; by this time he was gravely afflicted by Parkinson's disease. *www.iwm.org.uk/collections/item/object/80010197*

of humour'. And why was he known universally as Crackers? No less illustrious a judge of these things than General Sir Peter de la Billière, the commander of UK forces in the first Gulf War and one of Britain's most decorated soldiers, wondered whether it derived 'from the craziness of the daring which he had shown leading patrols in WW2'. Dad once confessed the truth to me. As a recently commissioned officer in the mid-thirties he had been the ringleader in some Bertie Wooster-style high jinks in Scarborough. Aware that the police had been called he piled into his car and drove back to Catterick Camp, where he was stationed at the time; on arrival in the mess, one of his terrified passengers announced, white-faced, 'that man is crackers'. The name stuck, most probably because it suited him so well.

Nothing really encapsulates his singular take on life better than the three conversations (all brief in the extreme) which covered what in those days was described as 'the birds and the bees', always delivered by one of your parents, in my case Crackers.

The first occurred when I was approaching puberty, and went as follows: 'Your mother wants me to talk to you about sex, but I'm buggered if I'm going to'.

Four years later, aged just seventeen, I was being sent to school in Germany, the Aloisiuskolleg in Bonn, for one term, a measure taken to try to ensure my schooling in England did not end prematurely (an ever-present danger, as you will discover below). As I packed my suitcase Dad sauntered into my bedroom, sat on the bed and extended his arm across the counterpane, concealing something under his hand, which he suddenly raised as if a conjurer. To my stupefaction he revealed a packet of twelve Durex. His only sentence was: 'Listen hard, son; please use these unless her surname begins with "von" or her father's an industrialist'.[2]

The third and final chapter of my paternal sex education came as I was just about to leave university. It was approaching dinner time, Mum was in the kitchen and Dad and I were having a drink in the study.

'Have you', he enquired politely, 'ever made love to a girl on a train?'

I spluttered not, somehow feeling that I'd let him down.

'Let me recommend the night sleeper to Fort William and in particular the points at Crewe,' my father responded quietly, as if this was a nugget of advice that one couldn't go through life without.

In such manner, I was always encouraged to enjoy myself. That wasn't to imply that there were not firm expectations and clear lines that I must not cross. Self-effacement was prized, good manners and what used to be termed common courtesy to everyone pre-requisites. I also have a keen memory that my father hoped that I might make the world a 'slightly better place'. But neither of my parents was so prescriptive as to tell me how this might be achieved. It was just left there as an aspiration.

---

2 I returned resolutely still a virgin two months later. I remember standing on the top deck of the ferry from Zeebrugge and chucking the packet of twelve overboard just in case I underwent a postmortem on arrival home.

My mother too was an enormous character, possessed also of a great sense of mirth. It fell to her to administer day-to-day discipline, a feature that I began to test increasingly. When I went through a prolonged bad patch, lasting quite probably a decade, she took it upon herself to tame the tiger that I must have resembled. But she was always loving and warm.

So with these as my guiding lights I grew up in a large house in Northumberland, on which nothing was spent for the three decades we lived there. It may not have been one of those houses where you put out buckets to collect the rain coming in from the roof, but it is true to say that the bathwater was never hotter than warm, and meagre in quantity. In other words, my early life was as close to genteel poverty as you could get. Two years above me is my elder sister Georgina, and three years my junior is Sarah. My recollection is of a house that was filled with noise, most of it joyous. We were an emotional bunch though, so there was definitely the odd stand-up row.

I firmly believe that I have been moulded by four people, two of whom were Crackers and Liz. The third was Tim Card, my housemaster at Eton, where I was sent in 1972. Whilst I was there my natural exuberance began to flower into pronounced wildness, and in earnest. Tim did his best to control and steer it, sometimes with exasperation wearing through his patience, but always with humour and humanity. It was Tim who had insisted on my attending Aloisiuskolleg, a choice that had been voluntary for others in my year who went, though not for me. In those days serious offences were met with beatings ('six of the best') from the headmaster. It was nigh on impossible to have this punishment meted out twice – you were then asked to leave. Somehow, though, I managed to exceed all the disciplinary norms, ending my time there as the most caned boy in the school by some measure.

Long after I had left, Tim astonished me with a story of my mother telephoning him one evening in despair at my antics. Her purpose in calling was to ask whether it was possible to have me beaten a little more often. Tim refused, with the parting piece of wisdom that: 'He may well be expelled, but I guarantee no harm will ever come of him'.

In 1977, having done far too little work to merit a place at Cambridge, my first choice, I headed off to St Andrews thinking I was going to study law, only to discover on arrival that it wasn't on the curriculum. And so in short order ended my prospective career as a lawyer. I instantly elected to read history, a wise choice as it happened. First, it was then and still remains something at which that great university (the third oldest in the English-speaking world) genuinely excels and, secondly, it inculcated within me an abiding love of the subject. Ever since, there has constantly been a history book, biography or memoir on my bedside table. Over the past forty years I have read literally hundreds. On the next page is a list of my dozen favourites, in roughly chronological order of subject matter, should you be in need of a good read.

The Mighty Dead ~ Adam Nicolson
The Hollow Crown ~ Dan Jones
William Pitt the Younger ~ William Hague
Of Living Valour ~ Barney White-Spunner
Napoleon the Great ~ Andrew Roberts
The American Civil War ~ Winston Churchill
The Great Game ~ Peter Hopkirk
Storm of Steel ~ Ernst Junger
The Seven Pillars of Wisdom ~ T. E. Lawrence
Appeasing Hitler ~ Tim Bouverie
Berlin ~ Antony Beevor
Vietnam ~ Max Hastings

Around the time of my twenty-first birthday, I was privileged to receive another nugget of 'Dad-ist' advice. Having watched him toil hard, rising at 5.30am each morning to earn the money to educate his son (who must have seemed determined to get himself expelled from wherever he was sent) I felt obliged to thank him fulsomely and to apologise. Upon my stuttered acknowledgement, he responded:

'What on earth are you talking about, dear boy? Listen, I never had any money, but I found it. Your grandfather was the same. And you will never have any money, trust me, but you too will find it.' Direct and prophetic in equal measure.

At the age of twenty-two, well into my fourth year at St Andrews, the topic of what I was going to do for a living was raised. I had not a clue. My father's only real experience was of the military and I had decided against that. 'How about merchant banking?' he suggested. From what little a Northern lad could glean it involved working twenty per cent harder than others for twenty per cent more money. But what appealed more to me was that it was then unarguably the most challenging area of the City in which to secure employment. The prospect of what this might do to my love life – there genuinely was a cachet in those days to being able to say 'I'm a merchant banker' – convinced me.

Somewhat to my own surprise (I confessed at the final interview to being no good at maths) in September 1981 I started my career at the then august house of Kleinwort Benson. A few years later the bank opened a small representative office in Dallas, Texas, where I was sent as the junior on the team.

During my time at St Andrews I had bunked off for a couple of days now and then to go fishing. But it was all too little and too infrequent to move beyond the most basic levels of proficiency, though I remember catching the odd unfortunate fish here or there. This changed in Texas, however, where I fell in with a family that was a by-word for Southern charm and generosity – the Kelloggs. In love with the frontier ideal they relished nothing better than to hunt (what the British might call shoot) game and to fish, and with a ranch in New Mexico and access to the properties of others belonging to their friends and neighbours I was, at last, given both the time and opportunity to explore what would become a real passion.

Though I had fished around a bit before (on average

never more than once a year), my angling diaries commence here in 1986. They tell the story of how fortunate I was, almost certainly without my recognising it. April saw me catch three rainbows spinning with a red and white spoon on a lake at the Philips Ranch in New Mexico. In July, I was back staying with the Kelloggs, and this time we stalked trout on the brooks of the Sangre de Cristo Mountains at the southern end of the Rockies. I recall being baffled and feeling inadequate, upstream casting being a complete novelty, but ultimately successful to my intense joy and relief.

Then, in August, I was sent to attend a cable television conference near Vail in Colorado. The agenda for Friday afternoon looked a bit dry (to put it mildly). So I played truant and hired a guide who took me to the Frying Pan River. Not only was I made to cast upstream on this beautiful water, but at that time of year the fish were only responding to a nymph, which of course sank. Again I discovered how inept I was, not least because I had no idea how to strike when the fly was taken. History does not record how many I missed; however, at a certain point my guide shouted 'strike' and I raised my rod. The result was a wild one-and-a-half-pound brownie.[3]

What wouldn't I give now to go back to those eye-wateringly beautiful locations with the benefit of experience?

---

3 I was surprised by this as I had thought all trout in the USA would be the domestic rainbow. However, at some point the Frying Pan River system had been stocked with the brown trout, native to Britain.

Prayer

'Keep your eyes on the stars, and your feet on the ground'
Theodore Roosevelt

On leaving the Army my father professed to have a desire to go into either politics or the church. My mother's only subsequent observation on this was: 'Thank God he did neither'.

Ours was not an overtly religious household. Indeed, other than at Christmas, Easter and weddings, I cannot remember Mum ever accompanying Dad on his weekly visits to church. And our own upbringings were typical of the schools we attended. They were all Church of England, and there would be morning prayers and Sunday services, but devout adherence was never demanded, or indeed expected.

At Eton we were offered each morning the option of

an 'Alternative Assembly' or a short service in College Chapel. It was a no-brainer really, but for a wholly secular reason. Whereas the timing of one's presence at the assembly was enforced ruthlessly, one could reliably turn up at chapel up to five minutes late and not be punished. This suited me well, as I was at this time of my life pretty much permanently in trouble, and tardy to boot. And it would appear to have the same appeal for a number of my peers; of the twenty or so boys who routinely attended there was a handful of comparable villains.

Over time, though, something else took hold. This was not a fervent faith, but instead a love of the graceful beauty of the surroundings, and an appreciation of the calm offered by the routine of the liturgy. And for the next four decades of my life I carried this with me, attending church about two or three times a quarter.

Upon my being diagnosed with cancer, Jill turned to me one morning and asked me whether I shouldn't explore faith, as a support. I'm not sure what she expected me to get out of it, and nor was I. There was certainly no vicar I could readily think of to help me. Of late I had become somewhat bemused with the quality on offer. Most sermons seemed to start in the vegetable aisle of Sainsbury's, and not improve in quality substantially beyond that.

And then I had a flash of inspiration in the shape of Jonathan Aitken. His is a name that requires little introduction to people aged forty or over. Whenever a politician is either disgraced or falls outside the law his name crops up. In 1995 he had found himself involved in a complicated spat with the *Guardian* when he sued the paper for libel, proclaiming himself ready 'to cut out the cancer of bent and twisted journalism in our country with the simple sword of truth and the trusty shield of British fair play'. However, in the course of the libel trial, he was caught out telling a lie about who had paid his £800 hotel bill at the Ritz Hotel in Paris two years earlier when he was a Defence minister. Charged subsequently with perjury, Jonathan pleaded guilty and was sentenced to eighteen months' imprisonment. He served his sentence in HMP Belmarsh – the first Cabinet minister to have been jailed since the time of the Tudors.

After his release in 2000, he studied theology at Wycliffe Hall, Oxford and was awarded a first class degree. He started a new career as an author, prison reformer and Christian speaker.[4] Our paths had crossed over our joint interest in rehabilitation and a somewhat distant friendship had grown.

So I telephoned him in late May 2013 and at the time of my biopsy he appeared in my room in the Cromwell Hospital. At the end of a wide-ranging conversation on my illness and what it entailed, and a gentle exploration of how any faith I might have could help me, he asked if he could pray for me then and there. It was a moment in which I felt deep emotion

---

4 In the summer of 2018 he was ordained as a priest and currently works as a non-stipendiary prison chaplain in HMP Pentonville.

and gratitude. Tears rolled freely down my cheeks.

My sense is that those afflicted with a terminal illness will regard religion in one of three ways. The first might be to retain a wholly agnostic or atheistic position. The second is to turn away from whichever deity they had previously worshipped on a 'how could this happen to me?' basis. The third is to draw great strength from a closer relationship.

My aim here is not to proselytise. Heaven forbid! But here's what happened to me.

I had been struggling with the nature of death, which had so suddenly opened up before me like a chasm. Of course it had always been there (the only two certainties in life being mortality and taxes), but was something I had never considered in an immediate context. Over the coming weeks, and with Jonathan's help, it was something that I found I had managed to get my head around. And that was a really, really big thing.

I have spoken with fellow sufferers whose approach seems to stem from a denial of the possibility of dying. This wouldn't work for me, necessitating as it does, a wilful optimism that doesn't allow you to look down. But the problem with a terminal illness is that sooner or later the bad news arrives. I found, though, that having looked down and accepted the potential imminence of my own demise, I was now ready to look upwards – to embrace optimism and fun and all the good things that life (however brief) can offer.

These days I am to be found back at Morning Prayer on a daily basis, most usually at St George's Campden

Hill in Notting Hill[5], led by the inspiring Father James and his team.

The ridiculous to the sublime, one might argue.

And since attending the funeral of a similarly eager angler I have adopted this prayer too:

I pray that I may live to fish...
Until my dying day
And when it comes to my last cast,
I then most humbly pray:
When in the Lord's great landing net
And peacefully asleep
That in His mercy I be judged
Big enough to keep.

---

5 Curiously, having lived within five hundred yards of St George's for the prior two decades, I only entered it for the first time in the summer of 2013.

My own personal Capuzzo:
June–July 2013

Why is it that we always put off those things that we dread most? You may not; I certainly do.

And so it is that this part of the story, which appears chronologically quite early on, was the very last chapter that I found myself able to write. However, it is all part of a consistent picture. Around that time I also bought the latest in the *Bootleg Series* by Bob Dylan; I revere the man and own more than fifty of his albums, but after just one listen I have never been able to face hearing it again.

And what makes it all the more surprising was that the operation I was about to undergo would (as it turned out) leave me completely cancer-free for two and a half years, and more or less happily cohabiting with the disease thereafter to the present day. Oh, and a firm and enduring new friendship as well.

Some details of the ordeal I have probably forgotten

whilst others are so firmly engraved onto my memory that they are as though I'm looking back at the events of last week.

I had then an overwhelming feeling of 'going over the top' to face the enemy. This was burnished by the lunch with my two sisters immediately before travelling to the Cromwell Hospital. The conversation seemed to veer away from everything save trivialities. A reflection of those hellish occasions that must have taken place a century earlier as the newly enlisted bade farewell to their families, I suspected. The weather didn't help much either – a slate grey sky with heavy cumulonimbus clouds threatening a downpour. I had desperate need of my father's courage and flair, to say nothing of grit and grace.

And the evening that followed, spent in the hospital on my own, appeared designed to depress. This was perhaps inevitable as I had to fast and they had to observe me for my operation in the morning. I'm sure that I have known greater misery in my life, but episodes do not readily volunteer themselves. In this frame of mind the arrival of the team taking me to the theatre actually served to raise my spirits.

Even as I write this, I blanch a little at how over-dramatic I was probably being. There was I trying to channel the sangfroid of my soldier relatives. They faced hideously high odds of dying whilst mine were close to zero. They faced real malevolence – I was surrounded by a team that was plainly exceptional.

Immediately outside the theatre I saw Loic, all scrubbed up and ready for action – oozing an infectious confidence. Then the anaesthetist hove into view. For some reason I turned to Loic, more or less on a whim, and said: 'If you get me out of this jam, we'll go fishing together'.

'Well there's something for us both to plan,' he responded. And after a hurried and inadequate farewell to Jill my hand was injected and I experienced those delicious few seconds of wooziness as you go under.

The operation I was set to undergo bears a little explanation, though I'll be careful not to bore you. It was pioneered by Loic in his days at Harvard. There are two noteworthy things about it for this story. The first is that it replaced a partial or complete removal of the affected lung, an operation that was plainly horribly intrusive and brought with it a very substantial risk of death – in around forty per cent of cases. And, secondly (but this only became clear to me much later), it is a procedure requiring inordinately high levels of skill on behalf of both the surgeon and anaesthetist. Scraping out the cancer sounds easy until you think that it's on the outside of the lung, which moves each time you breathe. In my befuddled state I did make a mental note of Loic's post-operative comment that he had pricked my lung a couple of times, but mercifully it had never collapsed.

Whatever my fears at the time, mortal danger was in fact remote. I came round fuzzily some six or eight hours later to be joined shortly by Loic and Jill. A triumph it was all deemed to be – everything removed and no signs of sarcoma.

And so began the drudgery of recovery – something

for which I was ill-suited. To begin with the pain was all-encompassing and ferocious. To cough was agony, to laugh overwhelming. And my lungs had to regain capacity. Slowly, tentatively, I managed to climb out of bed, though my mobility was hobbled by the three or four drains coming out of my side, from my lungs down tubes and into a bucket. When I undertook physiotherapy this got carried around by me – rather indecorously as I thought at the time.

I was incarcerated in the Cromwell in all for ten days that June. They always say that war is ninety per cent tedium and ten per cent terror, and that pretty much summed up my recuperation. There were one or two lighter moments. My personal favourite took place in intensive care; there was a button within easy reach enabling the patient to self-medicate with morphine as pain relief. When the light went green it was ready. Never one for instructions, I had misunderstood the nurse to be recommending that I press it whenever it went green. Only the following morning, when I was told that I had used a lot of morphine, did I understand my error; though this was not to be before experiencing a mammoth high, shortly to be followed by a proportionately sized hangover.

Just about the only other high was a blood transfusion – a sort of reversal of the previous experience; the slough of despond in advance of its arrival followed by a sense of calm elation.

To this day, whenever I'm asked if I'm allergic to anything I always respond in jest: 'hospitals'. This owes itself to my period of recuperation in the Cromwell, itself augmented by an additional three days from 30 June to 2 July, when I was brought in for observation following a return of some insistent and troubling chest pains. For a couple of hours I thought the entire inside of my body was in danger of collapse, though on reaching medical care it transpired that the problem had instead been caused by my having run out of pain killers. Those who have been in a similar spot will know that after major surgery one leaves with bags of pills, each having to be ingested at different times of day. It's easy to lose track of them all, and this is what I had done. A mistake you only ever make once ...

I have to think hard of days on a river that I haven't enjoyed, but it's safe to say that 8 July was one of those. On paper it looked like it was going to be an enormous success. The sun shone brightly, we fished in shirtsleeves, and Andy Murray had the previous day become the first Briton for seventy years to win Wimbledon. But all this was marred by the convulsions in my stomach. What I had failed to realise was that the painkillers, or opioids, I had been taking have as one of their side-effects constipation. In our family we use the euphemisms of a 'local call' or a 'long-distance call' to differentiate between what men do immediately after breakfast standing up or sitting down, respectively. Since my return from hospital eight days before I think it safe to say it had been local calls only and my body had now decided otherwise. An excruciating and lengthy process ensued. I withdrew to the facilities within the National

Trust-owned Mottisfont Abbey. Unfortunately there was only one gents there and, after my incarceration there for some forty minutes, I found myself fending off an irate member of the public who accused me of taking drugs and threatened to summon the police. If only he had known ...

The day was not without success, but even that was qualified. I did land one trout, but it was foul-hooked.

The family arrives: 1987–2002

I returned to London from the USA in 1987, and there succeeded in pulling off the second and probably only other clever thing I have done in my life.

On 12 August of that year, I went to see a play called *Serious Money*, a parody in rhyming couplets of the late-eighties financial world. This was the pretext for a blind date with a young woman who a university contemporary of mine, Piers, thought I should meet. Just before the intermission, the action wound down with a song specially commissioned from the legendary Ian Dury. Devotees of his, and particularly those acquainted with that magnificent song Plaistow Patricia, will know that some of his songs are not for sensitive ears, as was the case on this occasion. As we trooped off to find an ice cream and with my sides aching with laughter, I ventured to suggest to my companion that we were witnessing a masterpiece.

Coldly she replied that she thought it was awful.

Cutting my losses at dinner afterwards (surely the intention wasn't to pair me with someone so eminently unsuitable) I drank too much and ended up best of mates with the resident piano player. Only the morning after as I surveyed the wreckage in the mirror whilst shaving did I rethink my position. This young lady was plainly brainy, not to mention pretty and slim and elegant. But I'd blown it, and not for the first time. Feeling rather tired and blue I took a call from Piers: How did I think it had gone? Regretfully I reported back the position as I saw it. 'I'm not so sure,' was his only response.

And thus began my romance with Jill Langham, one that I'm happy to report continues to this day. To my everlasting gratitude, her many attributes also include energy, compassion and humour, all in generous proportions. But she has always been quick to get to the point of things. The early stages of our courtship frequently resembled a job interview (with MM as the candidate); at one point she announced: 'You'll ski!', something I had never previously tried. 'Fair enough,' I countered, 'but you'll fish'. That was effectively our only pre-nuptial agreement.

We were wed on 3 September 1988, less than thirteen months after *Serious Money*. Time has, I think, proved each to be an ideal foil for the other. And my, how we have laughed over the past three decades and more!

She is of course the fourth of that group which has

moulded me into the person I am, along with my parents and Tim Card.

At an early point in our marriage we agreed that at any part of our lives together one of us should be pursuing a sensible course whilst the other charged at something more unconventional. This first manifested itself in the rapid expansion of our household. Before this began in earnest, though, we endured a setback which was almost certainly the first trauma that either of us had ever suffered in our lives; in May 1990 our first child, whom we named Hugo, was stillborn.[6] This tragedy instilled in us a second realisation. We cared far more about children than any notion of economy. As a direct result, Jill then set about motherhood with determination and, given her drive and strength of character, the results were inevitable. In short order along came Lara in 1991, swiftly followed by Ivo in 1992, Paddy in 1994, India-Rose in 1995 and Honor in 1997; oh, and Daisy as a late and enormously welcome addition in February 2003.

In the meantime, I was being sensible and working hard in the City to pay for all this growth. But my heart wasn't in it, and in the increasingly cut-throat world that finance had become I kept being squeezed out of jobs. In truth, 'squeezed' is a sure euphemism for fired. However, my professional decline began to be offset by a rise in Jill's prospects. She had stopped working when

---

6 1990 and 1991 were testing years. In January 1991 my mother died followed in October by my father, only nine months later.

India-Rose was born, but, given the intermittent nature of my earnings and the number of mouths in the May household, had gone back to UBS[7] in 2001, permanently busy and travelling far and wide. One night over supper she opined that we couldn't both be bankers – there was simply too much to be done looking after the children. In less than five minutes I leapt at the chance to do something different.

At a previous crossroads in my career I had yearned for a life in the charitable sector. I couldn't explain it and couldn't then afford it, but the idea lingered; by late 2002, with little other professional option that was palatable, I leapt at it.

Whilst this was all going on, it was in this period of my life that salmon fishing truly got into my veins.

My diaries record that I had enjoyed two magnificent days in August 1986 off Vancouver Island. I was taking my holiday with my university chum Richard Mackie[8] and we had driven the hundred miles from his home at Nanaimo, staying in a primitive hotel in the town of Campbell River. Each of the two days we were taken out by a local guide in a fourteen-foot boat to trawl at the mouth of the river itself. It was proper August weather – the sea was glassy still and the scenery quite awe-inspiring. In this mode we happily spent our time,

---

7 Jill had originally worked for the merchant bank S. G. Warburg, which, whilst she was on semi-permanent maternity leave, became part of the Swiss bank UBS.

8 Very much in contrast to the behaviour in evidence that week, Richard developed into a formidable social historian, twice winning British Columbia's top award for works on the province's development.

drinking whisky by night and lager the following day to annul the effects of the spirits, and periodically something took the strips of herring we were using as bait. In total I reeled in eight fish, including four cod. The highlights though, and the reason we had made the trip, were the four coho salmon, averaging four pounds apiece.

This experience had stimulated my desire to catch more, and this time Atlantic salmon and in a river, rather than by trawling at sea. The decisive breakthrough came in the form of an invitation in June 1990 to stay at Delagyle on the Spey. This was owned by my old friend David Astor, and it was typical of him and his wife Marianne that he should respond so instinctively to someone else's misfortune.[9] In those days the great rivers of Scotland still enjoyed abundant runs of salmon and, sure enough, that week I caught my first grilse. The excitement remains with me vividly to this day. The weather was oppressive and grey and I was casting the line poorly in that most delightful of pools, Polmacree, being new to the fifteen-foot Spey rod I was using. Hooking anything seemed a very distant prospect as I made my way, a cast at a time, towards the tail of the pool, marked by a prominent pyramid-shaped rock. And then, all of a sudden, there was a sharp jolt; I raised my rod and was in. In what seemed a matter of seconds, though certainly was not, the fish had been netted. It

---

9 The invitation arrived by a hand-delivered letter before Jill had left the hospital at the time of Hugo's stillbirth.

weighed five pounds and was the first of many I was subsequently to catch on a Munro Killer. I retreated to the lodge feeling like a king.

And this first stay led to my taking a week's fishing in August at Delagyle for eight consecutive years from 1993. At its best we had enormous fun. In that first year, Jill caught her first grilse and, in 1996, we enjoyed our annus mirabilis, with the team of four managing seventeen salmon (at an average of nine pounds in weight) and seven sea trout. And, in 2000, I was treated to something magical. I was in Polmacree, the pool where I first struck lucky in 1990, and as I approached the tail I saw something large rising rhythmically. It was an otter, hunting. I stopped at a distance of twenty to thirty yards, stood stock still and watched. For about five minutes the otter continued its display, at points lying on its back before disappearing. Any fish in its right mind would surely have been put to flight but, as it was close to the end of the day and there was no point going elsewhere, I decided to finish the pool anyway. Imagine my surprise, then, when in the next thirty minutes I hooked and landed two fish in almost exactly the spot where the otter had been.

In the early years at Delagyle my inexperience was almost tangible. The key trick with this type of angling is to cover as much water as possible, and so the essential skill is to cast as much line as one can. Help is on hand in the size of the rod, but this heft is of little value unless you know how to use it. And that meant leaving behind what appears at first glance the easier style, namely the trout fisherman's over the shoulder cast, to a roll or Spey variant. This involves lifting the rod and rolling the line to form a tidy loop in the water at one's feet, and then flicking it up and out. Sounds easy, doesn't it? Well, it becomes so after days and weeks of practice. Once mastered though, there are few sights more graceful to my eye.

Reckoning ~ the start of a long process: September 2013

An important strand in this story concerns my first employer, the merchant bank Kleinwort Benson.

In early June 2013, it had been mentioned to me that there was a government compensation scheme for mesothelioma sufferers. I have written earlier that this is the only cancer that can be directly traced to a single source, namely asbestos. And it is almost inevitable that the afflicted individual cannot on their own protect themselves from it, most usually because they were unaware at the time that the particles they were inhaling were there. In other words, the illness is most often the product of negligence in the workplace. Given its deadly nature, the number of sufferers and the level of financial settlements (to compensate for up to thirty years of lost earnings and pension payments), a whole body of legal practice has grown up around this one disease.

The government compensation scheme exists to prevent vast swathes of the nation's construction and other industrial sectors from becoming gummed up in legal actions. Having worked in the charitable sector for a decade, the prospect was something of a silver lining to me as my overdraft was approaching its limit.

The claim form itself was easy to fill in, with what appeared to be an idiosyncratic request for a list of all the buildings in which one had ever worked. So, I dredged my memory and compiled the list, starting with 20 Fenchurch Street, the HQ of Kleinwort. On checking the form, I looked at the various addresses and, recalling the dark humour of junior employees all those years ago, on little more than a whim typed into Google '20 Fenchurch Street asbestos'. In under a minute I was reading an article in the trade magazine *Building* in which the demolition contractor, Keltbray, reported that it had taken a mere *seventeen months* to remove the asbestos when, in the early 2000s, they had pulled down the structure to make way for London's neo-futuristic tower known as the Walkie Talkie. Henceforth, I never doubted that this was where all my troubles started.

As I was soon to discover, however, demonstrating this fact was an altogether different thing. There are three factors requiring proof. The first is 'presence', of which we could be sure. The second is 'disturbance', as to reach the lungs asbestos has to be broken up into particles capable of inhalation. And the third is 'contact' – to demonstrate that I had been in the vicinity of circulating particles. And this was only thirty years ago ...

But the very first step was to find a legal firm to represent me. This work is always done on a contingency basis; that is, the lawyers bear the costs in professional advice and time. And mine was not an immediately attractive case, apparently. If you have precedent (such as loads of other co-workers previously compensated) or laboured in a place where exposure was almost certain to have taken place – for example, a shipyard or car plant – then demonstrating the three criteria is relatively straightforward. But I had neither factor on my side.

Since I had worked there, Kleinwort had been forced into the arms of Dresdner Bank, which in turn merged under duress into Commerzbank after the 2008 banking crash. This had never really concerned me, except that between them they had used an awful lot of lawyers, and I found myself declined as a client by one firm after another. I was now talking to Irwin Mitchell to whom I was drawn by their reputation in this field and their work representing thalidomide victims.

And so it was on an early day in September 2013 that I found myself on a riverbank on my mobile, arguing, pleading nearly, with the partner on the other end not to be 'conflicted out'. They had represented a company with an apparently similar name in the past few years. But that was after the Commerzbank merger when the private bank and the moniker itself had been spun off to some private equity backers; a completely different legal entity, I explained. Mercifully it was a late

September day with nothing rising, and a cold wind making me rather wish I was somewhere else; but it did afford me the time to put across my reasoning calmly.

After some thirty minutes or so I received a stay of execution. Rather than sack me, as was the intention of the telephone call, he would take it back to his compliance department and argue the case on my behalf. I didn't hold out much hope, and nor did I catch anything that day. But it was to prove the start of a long and happy partnership.

Three weeks later I became officially a client of the firm. Our relationship began with harsh and explicit warnings that they would drop me like a hot potato the moment they estimated the probability of success to be less than fifty per cent, and this was likely to happen reasonably quickly once the expert engineers had had a look at the case. If not then, when we had to set about proving contact. Paradoxically, this was the best possible start – from the autumn of 2013 on, I believed I had only a very small chance of success.

Why, then, did I pursue the case? It certainly wasn't the money; we never even discussed the likely extent of damages until two and a half years later. Nor was it a sense of burning injustice; I have always been quite forgiving of the mistakes made by Kleinwort's pretty hapless management.

Perhaps the answer to the question lies in an innate stubbornness.

Oncology and Sanjay Popat

Sanjay Popat is one of the central actors in this drama, though his connection to the river is tangential at best.

My introduction to him was unusual. The standard progression through the medical profession for a cancer sufferer is general practitioner, then specialist, then oncologist. The speed with which I had met Loic and the superfast road to biopsy and then surgery meant that chemotherapy, and therefore the choice of an oncologist, were ancillary thoughts. Not subsidiary, though, as events were to prove. We were given plenty of advice from a number of quarters, but the two that weighed most heavily were from Harpal Kumar, the CEO of Cancer Research at the time, and from Loic himself, each of whom impressed on us that if it were his father or wife, he would go for Sanjay.

An unintended consequence was that it drew us to

the Royal Marsden, where he is based. Over the coming years my respect and affection for this quite exceptional institution has grown and grown.

What struck me on our first meeting with him was his transparent humanity. He has a sweet nature, combined with a facility to get straight to the point. His approach is always analytical and driven by data, which some interpret as lacking in optimism. But, for heaven's sake, his specialism is lung cancer. The vast majority of his patients have only 'long months, rather than short years', as the cancer jargon has it; and peddling false hope is potentially cruel.

In short he is the yang to Loic's yin. I once asked Loic about their different approaches; he explained that surgeons are often miracle workers, and their operations the beginning and end of a relationship with the patient. This more often than not lends them an aura of optimism. Oncologists are best when they are realists.

Happily Sanjay combines these qualities with a gentle humour of his own and appreciation of others'. On our first meeting he advised me that the chemotherapy might render me impotent. 'My mother-in-law has been waiting for years for this,' I explained, 'we have six children already'.

'No problem,' he responded, 'we can always arrange an appointment at the appropriate storage facility'.

In early 2014, my first line of chemo at an end, I asked him to join me for a day on the Test. He politely refused, explaining that he was vegetarian, and avoided shedding blood. 'It's catch and release', I averred. He smiled but remained unmoved and I thanked him instead with brightly coloured socks, his Achilles heel, if you'll excuse the pun.

As our acquaintance has blossomed into friendship though, his understanding of what fishing can do for me has grown. A recent letter from him to my medical team concluded: 'He has no other symptoms of note, and will continue [on his current drug regime] returning in two months' time with the results of a further PET-CT[10] and reports of a planned fishing holiday in Russia.'

---

10 A PET (positron emission tomography) scan, in layman's terms, produces three-dimensional images of the inside of the body revealing activity in the patient's tissues and organs, and can often detect harmful activity, or the lack of it, before other imaging techniques.

Managing chemotherapy

Though countless thousands go through chemotherapy in any given year, including plenty of friends who can tell you what to expect, for each of us it is a unique endurance. Nothing can prepare you for the aftereffects of that first shot. Mine took place on 22 August, a brilliant sunny day, at the Royal Marsden.

In all, my cocktail of drugs numbered three[11], but it was one by the name of Cisplatin that was to be the cause of so much anguish. I had been warned of much but had no real idea what to anticipate. I thought at first that the impact would be immediate, so I repaired to bed on arrival back home. Much to my surprise, two hours later I still felt fine. In fact, it was only three days later, when I felt incapable of finishing my martini, that the toxic impact began to take its toll. And take it, it did.

---

11 Zemeta, Pemetrexed and then Cisplatin.

At various stages I felt lethargic, or giddy or just plain hungover (without the pleasure of having got there in the first place). Once I recall the pillow coming up either side of my ears as I lay in bed, simultaneously creating a sense of overwhelming claustrophobia and extreme nausea.

Overall, this period saw me fall prey to long bouts of torpor, which I came to describe as the 'tunnel'. I would enter it, and truly it felt like a gradual descent, on about day three of my treatment, to re-emerge some days later through some sort of ascent, equally gradual. And as with, say, the Blackfriars Tunnel, it was not pitch black in there; the overall sensation was of an unnatural illumination that sometimes strained the eyes. As we went through each infusion of the six in the cycle, the days spent in the tunnel increased, starting at around six and ending at nearly double that.

As it turned out, and as in so many other ways, I was fortunate. There were two contributing factors here. For the first time it became clear that my immune system was not normal, and in a good way. It is apparently extraordinarily rare not to be sick, by which I mean to vomit, as a result of the Cisplatin; a couple of months later Jill was sitting next to a physicist at dinner who flatly refused to believe that I had not thrown up routinely.

The second fillip resulted from a conversation with Jonathan Aitken, immediately prior to my first squirt of chemo.

'I do hope,' he said, 'you're going to be steady on parade'.

'What on earth do you mean?' I responded. 'I understand that I'm about to go through one of the more arduous experiences around, and you want me to keep a stiff upper lip?'

'Exactly so. If you are upbeat this will communicate itself to your children, who will respond by also being upbeat. Their demeanour will make you happier, and so you will have created a virtuous circle.'

This was possibly the finest non-medical advice I received in all the times of my illness. It is, of course, sometimes near impossible to put a smile on your face when the poison really kicks in. But, for anyone going through chemo, please give it a go.

And, in the third week of the twenty-one-day cycle, normal life pretty much returned. And thus on 22 September I found myself on the River Test at Mottisfont, fishing on the Rectory beat with my Northumbrian friend Richard Elliott. It was a perfect evening of Indian summer weather, and we were about to pack up. But there, opposite the hut, was a large shape under a branch on the opposite bank, rising to slurp down a fly every twenty seconds or so. A tricky cast, but that only added to the challenge, and thus the pleasure. And, on my second attempt, my fly landed in the perfect spot, a couple of feet above the last rise.

The result was worthy, dare I say it, of the effort - a fine four-and-a-half-pound trout. And a shaft of light through densely stacked clouds.

Making good on a promise: 26 May 2014

I had not really expected my surgeon to take me up on my invitation to come fishing, offered so frantically mere moments before going under the previous June. However, when I asked Loic again in early 2014 he accepted enthusiastically. Fully aware of how much I owed this man, I earmarked my most promising day, smack bang in the middle of 'duffers' fortnight', when the mayflies are hatching madly and the catching is commensurately easier.

This is a glorious time of year, and to anglers such as me the annual hatch of these large up-winged flies is a thing of wonder. Mayfly eggs are laid on the surface of the water and drift down to settle in gravels on the stream's bed, hatching into nymphs which live concealed beneath the surface for two years. In contrast to this, the airborne adult lives for just one day. When the time is right during May, the urge to hatch prompts nymphs to swim to the surface where, uniquely among insects, they shed their primitive aquatic casings suited for underwater life and emerge (hence the fly called the Emerger) as adult specimens called duns. They inflate their previously compressed wings and after a few cautious flaps take to the air. Having rejected their digestive systems, they cannot feed themselves and therefore waste none of the precious day on feeding. Later in their short span, they shed their coats again and transform into those magnificent and glossy specimens known as spinners. They are now at their best, ready for courting, and it is late afternoon.

At the height of the fortnight, the need to reproduce instructs vast numbers to mature simultaneously; large clouds of hatched flies can congregate twenty to fifty feet off the ground, where, dipping and swooping, they mate in a glorious dance. This achieved, the female returns to the water to lay her eggs and die. The cycle is complete. By dusk the water is frequently speckled with dead mayflies, their wings stretched out – thus another favourite fly of mine, the Spent.

Partly because of the mayfly's size and partly because this bonanza happens so early in the season, the trout gorge on them, rising steadily and with increasing frequency from around midday onwards. If you want a friend to catch something, this is the best time of year there is.

As I drove down to the Test I found myself a touch apprehensive. In the time since our initial meeting, I had formed a real fondness for Loic, but I had only ever seen him in a professional capacity. What would he be like at play, I wondered? This sense of nervousness was increased by a late request of his: could he bring along his father?

I need not have worried. Loic was at his exuberant best. In 2013, he had encouraged me onto a strict diet, the aim of which was to boost my immune system. Out of the metaphorical window had gone white flour, sugar, processed meats and most dairy products, including and especially cheese. So I was more than slightly surprised to be greeted with the gift of a runny Epoisses. When I challenged him gently his only response was that we all needed treats from time to time. The rest of the day continued in a similar vein. Though completely new to fishing, he threw himself wholeheartedly into the task and by the end of the day, and guided by Graham Wood, he had landed three trout, all on a dry fly.

His father, Gérard, proved a charming guest too. In his case there was an additional challenge to his never having fished; in spite of his career as a scientist, much of it spent in Canada (albeit Quebec), he spoke next to no English. This proved particularly exacting when he hooked a fish whilst I was looking after him. My French would improve as my treatments progressed but, in 2014, it had lain fallow for forty years since O Levels. Explaining how to raise the rod and then to keep the pressure on quite defeated me – all I could manage was 'tournez la roue', which was a desperate attempt to get Gerard to reel in some line. So often in life I have done everything right only to lose a fish, but on this occasion providence was on our side. Whilst not according to any plan and surely a picture of mirth to any onlooker, we eventually tasted triumph, and at a little over two-and-a-half pounds.

This day was the first of our days each year on the Test. As time progressed, Loic became more proficient and, I'm happy to say, even quite keen. Not that long ago he performed another feat of wonder on an acquaintance of mine, whose daughter, a Hampshire dweller, reported back to me that her father's surgeon spoke proudly of fishing 'regularly' in that county.

And more than finding a way of showing my deep appreciation for all that he has done for me, it also broadened and deepened our friendship in a way that only languid days on a riverbank can.

Approaching maturity: 2003-2012

'I never met a man who looked with such as wistful eye,
at that little tent of Blue that prisoners call the sky'
Oscar Wilde, *The Ballad of Reading Gaol*

The revival of my professional life occurred in a wholly atypical way.

In 2004 I was reading a paper on the criminal justice system and it led me to the conclusion that the way in which Britain treated ex-offenders was insane. The focus of this ire was the near impossibility of finding a job faced by recently released prisoners at that time. Two things about this struck me as barking. First, that having served time for, say, theft, the individual would then have to endure a second and effectively lifetime sentence of unemployment. Secondly, upon only a very small amount of research it became clear that many,

many ex-offenders desperately wanted to work (and by doing so to contribute to society) and society's answer was to deny those who knew how to break into our homes, or cars, or to sell drugs to our children, the opportunity to pay tax.

Having read further that a job cut the probability of ex-offending by about fifty per cent, my proposed solution was direct and simple. We were going to set up a company where you could only get a job if you had a criminal record. The statement itself was aimed as a direct reproof to us all.

And backed by the trustees of the charity I was then working for, Groundwork, that's what we did. To be honest, I never anticipated that it would go anywhere very far – the barriers at the time seemed immense. Would we ever win commercial work? If so, in which sector of the economy? Could we manage the ex-cons? And so on ...

Pretty much immediately I struck very lucky indeed. Then working for Groundwork was a man named Steve Finn, who I happened to know had been in prison. We sat down for a cuppa, and I asked him his story. Released after five years in prison in the early nineties, he was determined to go straight. However, this resolve was on the point of being tested after he had around one hundred and fifty job applications rejected at the point he disclosed his record. With Christmas approaching, he was about to do a little of what he called 'dabbling' when a friend offered him a job painting the railings in Kensington Gardens. He never looked back.

From having watched him in action I knew him to have formidable leadership qualities. Would he give up a sensible job to join me and my hare-brained scheme? Happily, he leapt at the chance. And there began a productive partnership, and a lasting friendship. His background was perfect – after the railings he had gone on to work in the Royal Parks for the best part of a decade. His knowledge of the grounds maintenance sector was vast and his commitment to a job well done absolute. And soon we had won our first contracts helping to keep the parks of Slough and Hillingdon tidy and were on our way.

To sum up the optimism we wished people to take from our social enterprise, we named it Blue Sky.[12]

At almost exactly the same time, my fishing fortunes also underwent a transformation. That this was so owes much to another character.

Robert Brydges was someone with whom I had worked in no less than three different financial institutions. A romantic and intellectual, in his youth he had been so in love with his postgraduate girlfriend that he in turn became besotted with Proust, her PhD topic. Following his published research in the early eighties, Robert is now credited with the discovery of the original

---

12 I had reread *The Ballad of Reading Gaol* and was particularly struck by the lines that open this chapter. I found recently the notes of an acceptance speech for some award or another won by Blue Sky. They read: 'Any mug can have a half-decent idea, but it takes an extraordinary team to make it a reality'. And so it was with Blue Sky, whose employees and trustees were quite out of the ordinary in their commitment. It might be wrong to single out individuals but Andrea McCubbin, our long-suffering COO, and Sarah Graham and Ron Sheldon, respectively our first and second Chairs, deserve special mention.

manuscript of *À la Recherche du Temps Perdu* – before then generally believed to have been lost or destroyed.[13] Why he went into banking is beyond me, but his role was to devise 'product' for people like me to flog. Around the millennium, his financial career had flagged, as had mine. I bumped into him in the street one day and asked what he was going to do. He was going to win *Who Wants to Be a Millionaire?* he calmly replied, and would I like to be one of his Phone-a-Friends. I told him he was bonkers.

Well, he was right and I was wrong. He was the third person to do so.[14]

Robert had moved down to Hampshire, acquiring Oakley Farmhouse at Mottisfont. It frustrated him that he was unable to fish opposite his house, as the owners, the National Trust, had granted the lease on the fishing to the subsidiary of a Belgian building products company. So he devoted about three years of his life to wresting it from them and getting it awarded to his new baby, the Mottisfont Fly Fishing Club, which, in 2005, enjoyed its inaugural year and prospers to this day.

Dry fly-fishing, casting upstream to a fish you can see and deceiving it into rising to the surface to take

---

13 See Brydges, R. (1984) 'Remarques sur le manuscrit et les dactylographies du *Temps Perdu*', *Bulletin d'Informations Proustiennes* 15, pp. 11–28; and (1985) 'Analyse matérielle du manuscrit du *Temps Perdu*', *BIP* 16, pp. 7–10.

14 At the time he won he was technically the fourth, having been in the studio waiting for his turn in the chair when Major Charles Ingram, the 'Coughing Major', claimed the prize. The latter was later tried and given a suspended sentence for 'procuring the execution of a valuable security by deception'. The conviction may be appealed following ITV's dramatisation of the incident in *Quiz*.

the imitation fly, contained any number of disciplines and skills I had just never learned. Not entirely surprisingly, therefore, I was completely out of my depth, and in that first season caught a mere four fish. But I was captivated – that was for certain. My summary entry in my fishing book noted:

'Overall a fabulous intro to the River Test and the dry fly. Plenty next year.'

In 2006 I caught twelve, still not a massive haul, but I was on my way ...

And indeed I did improve in the coming years.

One outing of particular resonance at Mottisfont took place two years later on 14 May 2008. My guest was a contemporary, Nick H-H, who had been grievously afflicted by multiple sclerosis since shortly after his fortieth birthday in 1998. For a couple of years before this he had been forced to use a wheelchair. This added an additional quantum of challenge to the task in hand and the elements were conspiring against us somewhat. It was bright and breezy and the water was cloudy after a week of rain. To offset this, we were helped by an early hatch of mayfly, though few were being taken on the surface – I counted a mere six all day.

The Rectory beat proved a beneficial setting though. First, we were able to access the centre of the beat by a field usually locked, but which the bailiffs kindly opened for us. Secondly, Graham was on hand to show Nick the ropes and to maximise his chances. A good thing too. Watching him learning how to cast brought home to me how this beastly disease was already affecting the strength of his arms. However, within a while he had mastered the basics and he and his wife were off with Graham, putting a Grey Wulff over likely spots. By lunch I was saying silent prayers that Nick would meet with success.

Mid-afternoon these were answered. I was downstream when I heard an excited hubbub. Running past the lunch hut I picked up my camera to record the forthcoming events. There followed a tense quarter of an hour. It was apparent that Nick had hooked a decent-sized brownie, and one which might have been a tussle for those in their very prime. But we three onlookers could all see how much this was testing his strength; with so many things that can go wrong anyway, I feared the worst. Still, nobody asked whether he wanted to hand over the rod, and I suspect his pride would never have allowed it. Back and forth went the line, and gradually the fight ebbed out of the fish, which held true to the fly.

And then it was at the bank for Graham to net.

The relief was palpable, and I remember looking up to discover each of the spectators dewy-eyed.

A long-term future for Blue Sky

My last infusion of Cisplatin had taken place in December 2013 but I started the New Year flat and exhausted. Gradually, however, over the next few months as the chemicals slowly drained from my body, my energy levels revived. I began to remember how normality might feel, though with the dull threat of the recurrence of my cancer always in the back of my mind.

With the arrival of the spring my spirits revived further. This has always been the season I love most. Rebirth, a return of birdsong and the colour green.

And this year there was the added bonus that I had moved up to a 'full rod' at Mottisfont, meaning I was going to have twice as many days there.

I also faced 2014 with a mission. We needed to find a way to keep Blue Sky going. At first sight this might have struck the dispassionate observer as an odd statement. Everything seemed to be going so well. In

2011, we had found ourselves as the chosen charity of the staff of 10 Downing Street and each year we seemed to win something at this or that awards ceremony. By 2013, the total number of current or former Blue Sky employees topped fourteen hundred. As an idea of scale, that is like going into a prison like Wormwood Scrubs and giving everyone a job. It's worth remembering too that we were the employer of these people, with all the responsibilities and challenges that that brings.

But behind an enviable façade there were desperate challenges. Winning commercial contracts was no longer the hurdle it had once been, and finding people to employ was straightforward. The true challenge lay in the pricing of those contracts. Work was plentiful if pitched at rates comparable to the market then – roughly £8.50 per head per hour. Pricing it more expensively than that would secure you nothing. But to run the whole shebang we needed roughly £12.00 per head per hour. This had never been an issue previously; we had secured funding to plug the gap from EU or government employment programmes, as well as from charitable foundations.

But, after 2010, the most applicable public sector initiatives dried up (a result of austerity) and we were thrown back increasingly on the great grant-giving trusts. At the same time we were growing, so the forty per cent or so of revenues required to balance the books was becoming a bigger and bigger figure. This had worried me prior to my diagnosis; it was one of my jobs to find this money (in the two years preceding 2013 this had risen to £800,000 each year, by some educated estimates roughly ten per cent of all grants made to the UK's criminal justice charities). Over time I had reached the pretty much inevitable conclusion that if the public sector wouldn't play ball (manifestly in its best interest but one should never underestimate the boneheaded obduracy of public sector policy and practice), the solution lay in merging Blue Sky into a larger organisation. Better that any day of the week than to watch the opportunity of jobs for those being released from prison disappear.

And so finding a permanent partner for my beloved Blue Sky became my professional purpose that year. And one which fully absorbed my energies in the four or so days I worked each week. I broke the challenge down into three pieces. The first was to secure a potential partner; the second was to sell it to the staff (one or two of whom seemed to feel more passionately about the enterprise than I did); and, finally, to sell it to the board (ditto). Although we conducted the process like the sale of a commercial company, there was one big difference; here there was no price around which to negotiate and then coalesce, and so everyone calculated what they thought might be the right deal by gut. This in effect meant feeling or emotion.

However, over the ensuing months the process worked itself through. Out of a shortlist emerged a preferred bidder, RAPt[15], with revenues about ten times

---

15 A wise abbreviation of the Rehabilitation of Addicted Prisoners Trust. In 2017, it chose to rebrand itself as the Forward Trust, an inspired name. Blue Sky as a 'brand' continues under its old trading name.

that of Blue Sky. Its sole aim in life was to get prisoners off drugs (without doubt the single biggest driver of crime in our country); as our objective of ex-offender employment was the biggest single factor in determining ex-prisoners wouldn't go back, the merger had overpowering logic. And RAPt was, I adjudged, an excellent ethical fit too (and five years later I'm happy to report that this, the most important thing of all, has proven true).

Finally, in October, after ten months of bashing away at it and managing a complex range of emotions (including and especially my own) the deal was done. Blue Sky, my baby, was safe. As time has gone by, the importance of this to me is hard to overstate.

Outshone and nearly defeated:
21 July 2014

It will happen to everyone who has children. That moment when they are better than you at your chosen thing.

My second son has always had a thing about the outdoors. In some ways, this is remarkable for he resembles neither his father nor his elder brother in turnout and appearance. A stylish, well-groomed type is our Paddy. But place him somewhere like Laikipia in Northern Kenya and you'll find him up before dawn building elephant fences or out with the rangers patrolling for poachers. Whilst there he even climbed Mount Kenya with the Royal Marines.

So it was no surprise that he should readily take to angling, and he has accompanied me increasingly. On this particular day, we were fishing on the Rectory beat at Mottisfont, which is seldom unproductive. The weather was glorious with a bright sun and little wind. The day will stick in my mind for two reasons.

One of life's most overused phrases these days appears to be 'size matters'. Accurate, of course, in many commercial settings, and I'm sure I have fallen guilty to the puffed-up pride in the aftermath of a particularly happy response from the piscatorial weighing scales. It is certainly true that in my downstairs loo pride of place is accorded to a picture of the three-hundred-and-forty-five-pound marlin I caught on Christmas Eve 1990.

But it's not always the case, as I was reminded on this particular day. It was all proving a little harder than I had eagerly anticipated earlier in the day. With the sun beaming down on the water, the trout had retreated to the depths and the shadows. And thus I found myself standing beside a footbridge casting beneath a tree. I had seen a number of rises there, never in one place, but spread about a bit. And just when I wasn't really expecting anything, it happened. Out of nowhere a dart, a splash, and something was there on the end of my line.

Now the vast majority of trout on the Test are stocked – known to the punters as 'stockies' or, more technically, 'triploids'. A bit of science here, perhaps. Triploids, as the name suggests, have three sets of chromosomes, whereas the indigenous brownies are diploids and have two. Having three sets of chromosomes rather than two makes the stockies infertile, and therefore unable to breed with the indigenous or 'wild' population. Each lives harmoniously with the other, with only the latter breeding.

Does it all make any difference? And how do you tell

them apart? Well, triploids tend to be larger because they have been reared and fattened up. Fisheries differ in the weight at which they release them, with our club tending to do so at two pounds while others may go for something slightly heavier, such as three or even four pounds. And the wild brownie in our neck of the woods is distinguishable by livid red spots on the lower half of each side; and, finally, it is almost always feistier.

And so it proved on this occasion. What had taken my fly, with quite some aggression, was in no time roaring all over the place. First upstream and then, to my consternation, downstream and under the bridge. Thus my rod was above the bridge and the line below it with the fish on the far side. If it was kept on the surface there shouldn't be a problem – over time the pressure of the rod will do the work and the line can be reeled in. But there was some weed directly below the bridge, and into it the trout sensibly swam. Stalemate.

Mercifully at this point Graham Wood sauntered up the bank with a broad grin on his face. There were two solutions: either to apply maximum pressure, though that risked breaking the nylon leader and leaving a glorious creature with a fly in its mouth; or to pass the rod under the bridge and, once downstream of the weed, apply tension and draw the fish backwards out from it. Whilst this might sound straightforward, it isn't and it wasn't. One end of the rod (the handle) is of course very strong, but the other is thin and susceptible to breaking.

To achieve the required handover, therefore, we got on our knees, one leaning one side of the bridge, and the other the other. A gasp from each of us and this most unusual of relay transfers had taken place.

A minute later and the fish had been freed from the weed, and sixty seconds thereafter had been landed. Truly a gorgeous animal, with bright scarlet spots. Quite possibly I blew it a kiss as I released it and watched it scoot off. Quite honestly, the catch of the season for me. Every time I cross that footbridge my mouth creases upwards in happy recollection.

And that would have been more than enough by which to remember the day.

But then came the rite of passage. We were driving home, Paddy and I, and swapping notes. I had caught one more besides, while he had landed three. With justifiable glee he asked:

'How does it feel to be second best, Dad?' I let it pass.

Five miles further on: 'Do you think you'll ever catch more than me again?' All gently done and in good heart but I would be less than honest if I told you that I was scarcely enjoying the banter.

And then: 'It's probably just an age thing, Dad. I wouldn't worry'.

I snapped: 'Listen, son, just shut the fuck up'.

For the next forty minutes there was total silence. 'Fair enough, Dad. I'm sorry'.

Harmony restored and peals of laughter. A gentlemanly and non-competitive sport?

The kindness of strangers:
25–27 August 2014

Overbidding on auction lots at charitable events can be both a blessing and a curse. Jill's habit of doing so, fortified by the odd glass of something or other, has certainly enriched our lives.

One such occasion was in early 2012, when she secured in the process two days' fishing on the celebrated Rutherford beat on the River Tweed. It all made perfect sense. The dates were for August, and that appealed as we had previously secured (in another auction) a week's stay at Fordell Castle, just north of Edinburgh. The plan appeared perfect, no matter that one lay only sixty-five miles from the other, a ninety-minute drive.

Except, sadly, it wasn't. On closer inspection the fishing dates were actually for the following year, August 2013. At the time this had appeared no great problem.

One year on, however, everything looked very different. By the time we came to schedule in my six rounds of chemotherapy, it became abundantly clear that whatever the state of my mental and physical fortitude it was unlikely to extend to standing in chest waders in a fast-flowing river.

So, with a heavy heart I telephoned the donor of the auction lot: could I possibly defer the days by twelve months? Asked why, though in a not unkindly manner, I provided my explanation, to which he promptly replied: 'In that case you must have a third day'.

And so it was that in late August 2014 Jill and I drove up to the Borders, for a half-week on the legendary Tweed, for many the spiritual home of salmon fishing.

I had not been up to Scotland for all of a dozen years, and in that time much had changed. Our timing proved interesting. We were into the final couple of weeks' campaigning in the Scottish independence referendum. South of the Cheviots this provided for some (usually thoughtful) press coverage, but the visceral nature of political debate up North had not been fully registered by me. Just sitting in the dining room of our hotel, the Roxburgh Arms, we were treated one evening to a be-kilted agent describing a substantial proportion of his fellow citizens as 'fat, drunken scroungers'. I was taken aback by the intensity and venom of his polemic. Of course, all of this and more awaited the wider country following the Brexit referendum two years later.

What had also changed were the general expectations aroused by salmon fishing. I had stopped going to the

Spey at around the turn of the millennium. The reasons were several, including the fact that as the children got older they drew less enchantment from picnics and the daily weft and weave of Scottish holidays in which they could not really engage. And it was a heck of a palaver moving up a family of our size. But the other principal cause lay in the disappointing catches I had experienced at the very end of the 1990s. My diary entry for the stay in 2001 recorded one brown trout and the comment 'thin week'.

And that year saw the last of our annual family pilgrimages to Scotland. My double-handed Spey rod had lain unused for some thirteen years. Getting back into the swim of things, therefore, took me some time. I remembered myself casting with no little elegance, but this was not how it looked in August 2014, at least for the first couple of hours. Gradually though, through trial and error more than anything else, and by my recalling that less is more, the line began to go out a little easier. All this is important – sometimes the élan with which you work the rod is just about all you can take away from a salmon river.

I had little expectation of catching anything, but just before lunch on the first of my three days at Rutherford I felt the unmistakeable jolt and tug of a fish taking my fly – the trusty old Munro Killer. Some minutes later and Michael Farr, the ghillie (or waterboatman as they call them up there) had netted for me a nine pounder. And, to my considerable delight, this was to be repeated two days later with a six-pound grilse.

My love of the pursuit of migratory salmon (and sea trout) had been rekindled. And, as subsequent chapters will tell, came to add an extra dimension to this story. Something I owe to the enthusiasm of my wife, and the kindness of a true gentleman.[16]

16 Thank you, Sir Christopher Lever.

Trout: 2015

When sketching out the skeleton of this book, 2015 appeared to feature little. My fishing diaries tell of some real highlights, but in the context of my medical odyssey it appears almost deafeningly quiet.

And so it was, pretty much. This was the only calendar year in which I was neither undergoing treatment, nor recovering from it. For if we're honest, in the first part of 2014 my body (and probably my mind also) was getting over the damage wreaked by that horrible drug Cisplatin.

However, against this backdrop of calm, some other big changes in my life were taking place. The one with the greatest impact was my retirement. In February I bade farewell to Blue Sky and to formal employment. This had been an inevitable consequence of the merger and I had had plenty of time to think it over. If I'm honest, though, I was dead nervous. I had worked constantly since leaving St Andrews and, having high levels of natural energy, I pondered much about the inevitable gaps that would present themselves in my days and weeks.

I think many had expected me to be appointed to the board of RAPt and, at the time, I was a little miffed not to have been, truth be told. As I write, however, I find myself eternally grateful that I was not. Had I been, I would have been unable to take a leave of absence from the minutiae; I would have been a nuisance, and would have frustrated myself and others. Instead, I am now able to look back on a job well done by my successor.

But what to do with my time? The medical advice was not to overdo it, which I took to mean an approximate working limit of three days per week. Another factor in my thinking was life expectancy – why saddle yourself with a job which would almost certainly not be as satisfying as Blue Sky when the conventional wisdom was that you might only have a couple of years of active life remaining? And there was always the consideration that even had I passed the interview the medical would almost certainly be beyond me. But deciding against a full-time post still left, as an option, consulting work. So I pondered this one hard; after all, I probably had experience aplenty in the charitable sector that people would pay for.

But, when I evaluated this one more fully, I kept asking myself the following question: 'How much money would I have to be paid per day to give up a day's fishing?' And the answer that I reached was that in the charitable sector, as a consultant, I would never have been able to earn what I perceived to be the threshold.

Of course, as time went by, non-executive trustee roles came along, which being non-paid meant that I remained the master of my diary. Only a dire emergency could bump a day on the river. In the immediate meantime I devoted myself to skiing (another story for another time) and, once that season had ended, to the prospect of an increased quota of time with a rod in my hand.

The stories from that year miss some of the drama of those preceding and succeeding ones as they lacked the interwoven context of medical developments. But they were eventful nonetheless. I had the same number of trout days as 2014 but it would appear that I made more of them, catching fifty-four (including grayling) as against forty-one the prior year; a significant advance in my strike rate, which at the end of that year had reached nearly three and a half fish per day.

A couple of days over that happy summer stand out vividly. I had been asked by Micky St Aldwyn to fish on the River Coln next door to his house, staying there overnight. It was a glorious stretch of water, around the size of a Test carrier, which he shared with a syndicate. Whilst his father was an avid angler, reportedly gutting and smoking his trout by the riverbank, Micky devotes his energies in particular to hard-core sailing. In spite of this, and as the perfect host, he joined me.

It was late May and the mayfly hatch was on song. The sun shone and my spirits were soaring. There were rises galore but, though I had a decent number come to my fly, they proved hard to hook. At the time I was perplexed, though was later enlightened by some sage that the further west one travels the quicker the strike needs to be. I am used to Hampshire, where too much speed can be a bad thing; in Gloucestershire, where I was, I proved just too slow. Hindsight is marvellous, even if the science is incomprehensible.

On the second morning, I was making my way down a stream with my host below me on the opposite bank. There was a fish rising insistently just below me. The flow was slow so I was able to cast down to it. Immediately it rose to the fly – a Mayfly Emerger, I remember – and I struck hard. There followed a procession of splashes and jumps as my line disappeared. It is not always clear at the outset the size of the quarry. Micky, who had sauntered up, observed that this looked pretty large, but my only concern was not to lose it, and therefore I played it with great respect. Rightly, as it turned out. At five and a half pounds once safely landed, it was the heaviest fish caught on that beat thus far in the season. Only three times in my life have I ever caught a trout of the same weight, but never more, and never before.

Tackle-tackle: July 2015

The idyll that was 2015 was enhanced in July by my first visit to Iceland. The triumphs of the previous year on the Tweed had truly whetted my appetite for more salmon. And thus it was that on 2 July my elder son Ivo and I set off for Reykjavik to 'the land of the ice and snow [and] the midnight sun, where the hot springs flow', as Led Zeppelin sang so memorably.

I had reviewed the options and, outside Scotland, they seemed to break down into three: Norway (very expensive), Iceland (less so, though still pricey and eye-wateringly beautiful) and Russia (excellent value for money but maybe a bit rough around the edges). Rather hoping that Jill might accompany me I had plumped for Iceland, though immediately on booking she found other more pressing things to be doing. Paddy, the only real fellow angler within the family, was otherwise engaged and so I approached Ivo who, contrary to my expectations, leapt at the opportunity.

After a culturally rich evening in the capital city, we had a morning to kill before setting off on the two-hour drive north to the River Nordurá. Discussing our plans at breakfast, Ivo's sense of humour was tickled by the prospect of the world's only phallological[17] museum and he put in a strong plea to visit. I was happy to indulge this so long as I in turn could drop in on a fishing shop to seek advice on the best flies (it really is amazing how gullible we fisherman are). 'So it's tackle-tackle, Dad', opined my son.

The drive to the lodge was a treat in itself, as the terrain became more hilly and remote, like no other place on earth that I had visited. I became terrifically excited on seeing an Arctic tern, a real rarity for most of us in the UK. I was to discover over the coming days that in Iceland it is as common as a blackbird. The sense of romance built on arriving at the lodge and meeting our guide, Einar, who looked like nothing other than a Viking with his strong frame, tattoos and enormous beard.

And thus we settled down to the next six half-day sessions. Each was six hours long, the morning beginning at seven o'clock, and the afternoon running from five till eleven in the evening. We ate dinner at midnight and sank into bed truly knackered an hour or so later. Not that it was ever dark, in my recollection. Our quarters were, in truth, far from luxurious, and sharing a room with my son I found to be an adventure in itself.

---

17 Look it up if you're not sure of its meaning!

Crackers, Mick and Liz May, September 1966

Graham Wood (left) and India-Rose landing a trout, 3 June 2013

MM, 1976 (and looking uncharacteristically demure for the time)

Clockwise from above:
Lara aged 10; Ivo aged 8; Paddy aged 7; India-Rose aged 5; Honor aged 3; Daisy aged 2 with Muffin

Images courtesy Hugo Burnand

MM (right) on the Sangre de Cristo, 1986

Jill, October 1987

Nick HH and his fish, May 2008

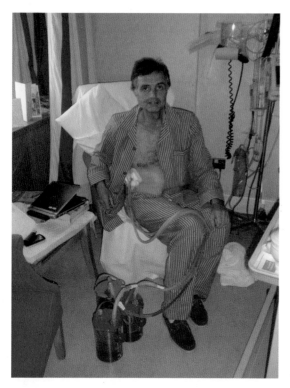

20, Fenchurch Street

MM in hospital, June 2013

Dealing with chemo – MM and Richard Elliott, Mottisfont September 2013

Professor Sanjay Popat

Graham Wood (foreground) and
Professor Loic Lang-Lazdunski
landing a trout

MM and Mark Sater, Salcombe Harbour, August 2018

(l-r): Daisy, Honor, Ivo, MM, Jill, Paddy and Lara,
29 September 2018 (sadly, India-Rose was travelling)

Image courtesy Hugo Burnand

Jill speaking, 29 September 2018

Image courtesy Hugo Burnand

MM in Tierra del Fuego, 2019

Sunset on the Rio Grande and a fish in the net, January 2019

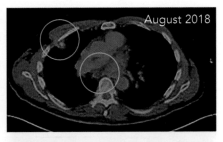

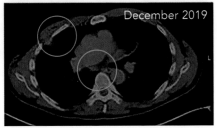

The impact of Vismodegib - MM's scan results (red spots = active tumours)

Jill and MM, Salcombe, October 2018

The 'Happy Man' – Varzuga, May 2019

*(l-r) Ivo, Honor, Mick, India-Rose, Lara, Jill,
Daisy and Paddy, the Grenadines, 2018*

Nothing had quite prepared me for the variety and majesty of the landscape and its colours. And this was vividly brought home to me the following day when, in bright sunlight, we crossed the crystal-clear waters immediately above the Laxfoss waterfall. We were about twenty yards from where the falls themselves plunge some forty feet onto the rocks below. I tried to take it all in as we linked arms, Einar, Ivo and I, lest any of us slip. And it was here that a critical element of the trip happened, as Ivo hooked and then landed his first, quickly followed by a second, salmon. A moment of true exhilaration for us both.

There were many and other highlights. What sticks in my mind are variously a near-tame family of ptarmigan scuttling through the undergrowth, the chicks smaller than a child's fist, the smoke rising from a thermal spring only yards from ice-cold water and the puerile jokes the three of us shared on the bank.

And, of course, the sport itself. By the end of the three-day stay, we had landed nine fish between us. Most were four to six pound grilse but, on the single-handed rods we were using the majority of the time, these felt plenty big enough. On two occasions we found ourselves using my big Spey rod, each with better than satisfying results. Unable in one pool to reach the lies with a single hander, Ivo tried and in thirty minutes of Einar's expert tuition mastered the cast sufficiently to land his third grilse, something I witnessed camera in hand from a cliff sixty feet above him. And I was privileged to catch the only fish caught that week above the falls; and, at nearly eleven pounds, the heaviest.

So we returned home weary but exultant; not a care in the world.

The medical outlook was not entirely cloudless, however. In 2014 and 2015 I was scanned quarterly. These were followed by consultations with Sanjay Popat. In my life, I have felt before the sense of numb dread that one experiences before an event that you know is going to be painful and cannot be avoided. Waiting to see the headmaster at school before a caning was a classic example. But nothing ever came close to the dry mouth and dull thump of the heart that was my lot in the waiting room of the clinic at the Marsden. Whilst I knew that the fateful day when we would discover that the cancer had returned would arrive at some point, thus far at least our meetings with Sanjay had always ended with a reprieve.

I always asked for a duplicate disc of the scan to take to Loic. This was an unorthodox modus operandi, but he offered all of his patients what he termed a 'lifetime warranty', apparently free at point of delivery.

A couple of months after Iceland he wrote me a letter in which there was an oblique observation to an uptick in activity, if not an actual growth, in my tumour. There was also a reference to the potential need in the future for 'treatment with platinum'. That passed me by for a couple of days, until I googled the constituents of Cisplatin.

Suffice it to say, I was on notice, and would remain so for the balance of the year.

Reckoning ~ the end of a long process: April 2016

Throughout 2014 and 2015, the pursuit of Kleinwort had rumbled on, picking up in intensity.

To begin with the task had been truly daunting. Over the past thirty years the workforce had turned into something of a diaspora; tracking them down with my limited address book looked as though it was going to take forever. Then two of my contemporaries[18] rode in with their contacts, and suddenly I was corresponding with forty or more former colleagues. But what were we looking for? And how many of us anyway could remember anything of value three decades or more later?

But slowly, often glacially, we started to piece

---

18 Jonathan Baird and Robin Hindle Fisher, to whom I'm indebted.

together the beginnings of a picture. Two critical steps were made in early 2014. The first was the independent surveyor's report confirming the enormous extent of the asbestos usage in the building, that it was sprayed (i.e. likely to become unstable) and of the worst sort, 'brown'. Secondly, we established that in 1983-84 the company undertook a major renovation of the building, expanding from the original lower ten floors to take over all twenty-three; this work was done *without* moving out the workforce. I had long remembered this, but had failed to spot its importance. However, from this moment on, we were clearly able to demonstrate unquestionable disturbance (of the asbestos) whilst I had been in the building. It was at this point that I perceived that the confidence of Irwin Mitchell in my cause became established.

But the distance to be travelled was still enormous. How on earth could we establish that I was anywhere nearby any disturbance? As my two-person team, the estimable Ian Bailey and Jo Jefferies, never failed to point out, any half-competent barrister would demolish my case in a matter of moments without that link.

My contemporaries, however, proved keen to help and so began a process of triangulation between me, them and the lawyers, and through the latter to the structural engineers. Various likely explanations and locations were posited. How about the safe in which bearer bonds and other valuable documents resided? How about the lifts? Where had I been when the renovations were taking place?

People have been kind enough to say I have a great memory, but there were chasms in what I could recall. And it all took so long – well-meaning people would come up with theories which we needed to run by the experts, and vice versa. The volume ebbed and flowed but in hot periods I might be spending up to three hours a day – some fifteen a week – batting stuff to and fro.

My view of the legal profession was to change profoundly. When I was first told that my action would be pursued on a contingency basis the phrase 'ambulance-chasers' came to mind. You know, those firms who advertise on daytime television. As time went by I learned the opposite was true in my case. First, I was told at the outset that I had a low chance of success. Then, and I only found this out very much later, at an early stage one of the most senior QCs in the land had advised Irwin Mitchell that the case could not be pursued successfully. It is therefore understating it to say that it is to Ian's and Jo's very great credit that they disregarded the advice, in spite of this becoming one the most complex lawsuits the firm had ever taken on.

In other words they believed in me, invested in me (and mightily in hours and the costs of the external engineer) and shared the risk with me. Therefore, I shall always be grateful for their commitment to the cause; at this time it was not unusual for me to receive emails from either of them sent after nine or ten o'clock the previous evening.

But all the while I was mindful of our relationship. When you engage a lawyer on standard terms it's very much he who pays the piper calls the tune. I may have been the client here, but I wasn't bearing the cost so I could only push Ian and Jo so hard lest they take the view that I was too much trouble and drop me. So there were weeks when practically nothing happened as they were busy on other cases.

However, as time went by, the charge sheet began to build. A former departmental manager gave a witness statement recounting a meeting during the renovation of an operations committee (of which we would otherwise have been unaware) at which confidential papers on asbestos had been distributed and then (highly unusually for that time) collected for shredding at the conclusion of deliberations. The engineer discovered that the Health and Safety Executive had written to the board of Kleinwort in 1976 (when I was still a schoolboy!) warning of the inherent dangers to the staff of the asbestos in that building. Though compelling, I thought, these remained straws in the wind; we still lacked anything resembling a killer punch.

As if by osmosis our team's eyes started to focus on the stairs, which I had used extensively over many years. This was a function of my somewhat individual duties, sometimes running up and down ten floors to collect approvals or documents, preferring this route to the lifts, which were always too crowded and therefore too slow. And, in the second half of 2015, the first of two or three heavy blows were landed on Kleinwort's case. In a contemporary and routine report on the renovation, our engineer identified a record of a couple of asbestos leaks on the tenth floor near the lift shafts and one of the two staircases – telling, though, without establishing that I had been there or thereabouts, not yet a knockout. Then it emerged that one of my colleagues had kept a desk diary detailing such things as office moves; these placed my department close to the floor on which the leaks had occurred, both above and below (we all moved offices quite a bit in this period).

The Holy Grail of these investigations comes in one of two forms. The first is the presence of 'men in spacesuits', i.e. protected removal specialists; the second is a pile of suspicious white dust or debris. The former never materialised but around this time the latter did, in a statement from an old boss of mine.[19] In this, he remembered in the late seventies a pipe bursting overnight above his office on the first floor and there being a pile of white dust on his desk. This was before I started work so the timing may not have been an exact fit. But, highly significantly, it was before any disturbance caused by the renovation work (thereby establishing that leaks had taken place even before the 1984 works had got underway) *and* I had worked on that floor for most of my four years in London with the firm.

But there was a hitch – as there always seemed to be. Just as we thought a settlement was in prospect it emerged that Kleinwort had insured its liabilities with not one but two insurers; the first appeared ready to take a reasonable line, but not the second. This, then,

---

19 Duncan Goldie-Morrison, another to whom I'm indebted.

led us into the first of two set pieces that were to draw a line under the whole affair.

The first was what is known as a commission hearing, effectively a court hearing but taking place with all legal trappings in one's home, recognising the incapacity of most plaintiffs in such cases. So on 14 December 2015 into our kitchen piled solicitors from our side and the defendant's (Commerzbank), Harry Steinberg (our silk), and John Williams[20] (theirs), as well as a notary and a judge. I was examined by Williams under oath, and though sympathetic in manner, he pulled no punches. At one point he argued 'Mr May, may I put it to you that that is a supposition'; I countered 'I believe that assertion is itself a supposition'. I saw the merest hint of a raised eyebrow from the judge. The hearing was probably a score draw and there was certainly no hint of a settlement in the ensuing weeks, but Steinberg felt convinced they would prefer not to put me in the witness box, should this go to court.

And then, at the turn of the year, there came something of a bombshell, or perhaps more accurately the setting off of an unexploded bomb. My scan in January 2016 revealed the cancer had returned. So it was back to chemotherapy, though this time there was less optimism around. Jill and I were both shell-shocked by the suggestion that I needed to make the best of the coming year ...

---

20 The website for his chambers advertises: 'He is extremely approachable, highly intelligent and a ferocious cross-examiner'.

And so Jill did what she always does best. She made things happen. The evidence had developed by this stage from former colleagues and an expert engineer who had carefully reviewed it all, and we were better placed to push hard for an arbitration meeting with the insurers. I am told that there is no obligation upon insurers to agree to this step, but after a couple of months of shilly-shallying we sat in the chambers of one or other of the QCs in Lincoln's Inn. In one room was our side, including Harry Steinberg, and in another room the two insurers and their collected legal teams. The way it worked was that Harry would take instructions from us and then meet with the other side in their room. I recall feeling more than a little drained from the chemo, but ready for the fray.

Our team debated first what financial settlement amount we should seek, the only occasion on which we had ever done so; I was firmly of the view that we should force the insurers to open the bidding. Half an hour later, Harry Steinberg re-entered the room with their first offer – fifty thousand pounds higher than the minimum Jill and I felt we could accept. There was an audible exhalation of air; we all knew then and there that this case was going to settle. Back and forth we went for a couple more hours, the figure slowly rising, when the defendants made what they said was their 'best and final offer'. It was a slightly strange looking number, and our advisers suggested we seek to push them up by nineteen thousand pounds to a round number. Again, I put my foot down. We had achieved a settlement well in excess of our minimum – why jeopardise that after all our hard work and risk a court case?[21] So we signed, and I remember John Williams, their QC, coming in to shake my hand shortly thereafter (I have often wondered how much I owed to his judgment).

So, what was the number? The honest truth is that I've now forgotten. That's not because I am so rich that it didn't matter – far from it. But it is testament to the fact that this was never about the money – it was about the principle.

And, for that reason, I am proud to have brought the action. For I may have been the first to have made the link but, subsequently and very sadly, there have been more sufferers identified – and at least one who has succumbed to the disease – who had previously worked in 20 Fenchurch Street.

---

21 Cases settled by arbitration ('on the courthouse steps') lack the drama and excitement of an actual court case, with berobed judges and imposing settings. But the consistent advice, and it was wise, was that we should do everything in or power to avoid the crapshoot of a formal hearing. There are just too many uncontrollable factors; a witness might not perform well under interrogation or the judge might be having an off day, by way of examples.

A better day than might have been:
20 June 2016

G iven that I was in the late stages of my second line of chemotherapy, the early part of the 2016 angling season had shaped up pretty well. The surprise in many respects was that I had managed so many days: five in all by the end of May, and my fishing diary reflected that in a range of weather conditions and a pretty moderate hatch of mayfly I had landed fifteen brownies, two rainbows and a grayling. All very satisfactory.

The medical, rather than piscatorial, explanation for this score is worth relating. The cocktail of drugs infused in the first line of chemo I had endured (between late August and December 2013) was different from that between January and June 2016. The critical variation was the replacement of the drug Cisplatin with another called Carboplatin. The former is marginally more effective, but at a cost of being massively more toxic. I was only made aware of Carboplatin in January 2016, when Sanjay Popat proposed it saying quality of life was probably more important than a percentage point here or there of efficacy.

But what next, now that the chemo was finished? There was some doubt as to whether it had had any impact at all, other than possibly to have held up the advance of the tumour. Thus, I had been advised this was likely to be my last ever line and we were urgently casting around for options.

This was a cause of anguish for me. However, and not for the first time, Loic Lang-Lazdunski rode to the rescue. The population of the medical world in the specialist area of mesothelioma is not vast. Loic had an old friend and colleague, Professor Arnaud Scherpereel, who was based in Lille. There he was running a trial of two immunotherapy drugs at the university hospital centre, the Centre Hospitalier Régional Universitaire de Lille (CHRU for short); would I like my name to be put forward?

The only problem, as far as I could see, was that the sole date Arnaud could do for a preliminary consultation was 20 June, when I had an appointment on the river. When we learned of this great opportunity we were staying with friends, who heard me negotiating with Jill to find another date. They agreed with her that I needed to grow up and give the fishing date away.

And so it was on that date that I travelled for the first time to Lille by Eurostar. Without knowing that he was talking about immunotherapy or how it worked, Loic had first told me about such wonder treatments three years earlier. Now, as if to emphasise the rapid and radical strides being made in some branches of cancer treatment, here I was hoping to be enrolled on a trial. Such an opportunity is something desperately sought after by sufferers of complex cancers. For these, conventional chemo is well known to keep things only at bay and for many the only route to a longer period of living is through drugs that have yet to be approved. As such, I was immensely fortunate and, in spite of my irritation at losing out on a day on the Test, I knew it.

I carried with me a disc of my latest PET scan, and was soon being subjected to the administrative bureaucracy at which French hospitals are so adept. I was enrolled as patient number seventy-three out of a total available complement of one hundred and twenty. There was very considerable concern as to my status as a British national, one of only two ever to be admitted (the other also being a patient of Loic's). After X-raying and the standard weighing and so forth, I was met by Arnaud. The first thing I noticed was that in comparison to all the nurses and admin staff, who only spoke French, he spoke faultless English, sexily accented according to Jill. This was the product of his having studied in Pittsburgh over a number of years.

He was determined that I should be admitted, notwithstanding the doubts as to being English, and signed me on. He urged me to get a European Health Insurance Card in the hope that this would resolve the cross-border funding issue. I got away with it for the first two or three visits, but it was to prove unsuccessful in making the problem go away, and I ended up funding the cost of the hospitalisation (happily though not the drug) at €859 per day. Arnaud's parting words at the conclusion of this, my first meeting with him, were 'of course, Mick, if the UK votes to leave the EU in Thursday's referendum I cannot say what will happen'.

I had not even considered the possibility that the EU referendum, which was taking place three days' hence on 23 June, would have any bearing on my treatment. But Arnaud's words were to have a fundamental impact on the voting patterns of la famille May. I have never been prescriptive in how my family votes, only that they do so. And, indeed, both before and after the referendum (and in contrast to so many others) we avoided impassioned discussions on the subject. But what conversations we had had revealed that we had four prospective 'remainers' and three 'leavers' in the family. When we did a postmortem in the aftermath of the referendum, we found that Arnaud's pronouncement had altered that balance to six:one in favour of remaining.

And who was the one who had voted to leave? Well, strangely, it was me. I'm afraid there are many things in the world I've never been able to look at without an overpowering urge to raise two fingers, and the European Union was a prime target.

But, back to the beginning, that day on the Test I was forced to give away against my better instincts I gave to Graham Wood. The sun shone bright, it was way too hot and one of the Test's most experienced ghillies caught nothing. Though not for him, all's well that ends well.

Expectations upturned: July 2016

One of my prime preoccupations whilst in Lille on 20 June was to ensure that my planned repeat trip to the Nordurá remained on. As soon as the ground rules for the 'MAPS 2' trial, as I quickly discovered it was called, had been explained to me I knew that diary management – never my strongest suit – was going to become an ever-present and urgent concern. The routine to which I had signed up was an infusion every other Thursday in France. This could be done by the day. However, there was also a requirement for a blood test forty-eight hours in advance (i.e. every other Tuesday). This could be done at the Marsden, or indeed anywhere really[22], but the combination meant that every other week had to be blocked out for Lille trips.

---

22 In my time I have had blood tests in Klosters, Kelso and Fort William, destinations that speak happily to the places I had visited.

To my intense relief, my first shot of Nivolumab[23] was agreed for 7 July. That itself was a mild blow – I had a day booked on the Test – but preferable by a substantial margin to the following week, which would have meant missing out on my much anticipated second visit to Iceland.

It also meant that we could still go to Delagyle on the Spey to stay with David and Marianne Astor. I have already written about my enormous affection for this place, and it was a pleasure that was set to be doubled for being accompanied by Jill and our youngest daughter, Daisy. But as I flew up I had no great expectation of actually catching anything. This is not meant to decry the invitation; the Astors being among my oldest and dearest friends. And indeed the first night, a Sunday, we set about our enjoyment with quite some abandon, leaving me with something of a headache the following morning.

In spite of my successes on the Tweed two years prior, I must confess that I had discounted almost to zero the probability of ever again landing a salmon in Scotland. This was in part reinforced by my experiences of the previous year on the Nordurá, where fish appeared abundant and therefore a stark contrast.

There was also an element of expectation management going on. Because I was off to Iceland the

---

23 The aim of MAPS2 was to test the efficacy of two immunology drugs, Nivolumab and Ipulimumab. The trial involved one hundred and twenty-five patients; sixty-two (including myself) were treated with an infusion of just Nivolumab and sixty-three with an infusion of the two. I was disappointed not to be in the latter group, but it may have been a lucky escape; sadly, I believe three of the sixty-three patients developed fatal side effects.

following week, I had persuaded myself that I really couldn't care a hoot as to whether I struck lucky on the Spey. I was there for the sheer joy of revisiting happy times in the best of company.

And this proved to be a wise decision at the end of the first day. I had been in the bottom pool on the beat, the Gean Tree, a spot of real beauty and past successes. My line had suddenly tightened and for some five seconds or so the reel slowly clicked. I lifted my rod tip … and then nothing. So that was it. I'd travelled to Scotland only to lose a salmon. Ah, well. That was typical of so many of the tales I had heard recently, and there was always next week …

But yet, but yet. The following day I was standing on the concrete embankment at Delene, as legend has it the most fecund spot on Delagyle. I was talking to the new ghillie, the low key and charming David, about his recent retirement from Scottish Power.

My hopes duly in check, then … BANG.

No reactions to manage this time, for the line was going out rapidly. Somewhat in trepidation fearing a repeat of the prior day, I lifted my rod and still the line was disappearing from the reel, albeit slightly more slowly. On a couple of occasions the fish even broke the surface jumping, but mercifully the hook stayed fast. Some ten minutes later a fresh and strong specimen had been landed, and returned to the river.

'Go on, Mick, admit it,' observed David immediately afterwards. 'It's easily the best fun you can have with your trousers on.'

My first trip to Lille was memorable for a couple of reasons only. The first was the journey; this was to become a routine, but the initial attempt at anything, particularly one starting so early in the morning, is always an adventure, I find. Secondly, there was the necessity to get the treatment without being clobbered by French bureaucracy, which I feared – wrongly as it turned out – might turf me off the trial. As it happened, both were negotiated successfully.

The following Tuesday I set off with Paddy on our Icelandic voyage. The sun shone as we left Heathrow and met us at Reykjavik too. The taxi driver on our way into the capital from the airport broke off from his discussion of Premier League football and the most recent European Championships to opine that the weather had been unusually pleasant, with little rain. This didn't bode well for the expedition upon which we were embarking, and explained the blog I had read a week previously telling of an extraordinary early run on the rivers.

As in the previous year, we visited the tackle shop to ensure the best supplies. This year they were recommending much smaller flies. These come in a range, as you might expect. The largest are size two (whoppers designed for heavy water) and in 2015 we had used eights and tens – standard fare for Scottish rivers in the summer and early autumn. Here we were being recommended twelves and even fourteens – the sort of size one might use on the Test.

If you have never visited a stretch of river before, there's a more or less infallible guide to its ideal height.

If you can see no rocks at all, then the water is probably too high; conversely if you can see a plethora on either bank and in the middle of the flow, the levels are probably too low. As we drove up to the lodge it was this latter sight which greeted us. Also on hand was the Icelandic agent, who, with the natural bonhomie of the middle man, confirmed that we needed to dig out our smallest flies. At the back of my mind formed the thought that this might not be the most stellar of trips.

This was amplified by our evening sally immediately afterwards. First, we were allocated a local guide whose English was execrable – a true rarity in Iceland. Then, at our first pool whilst showing Paddy where to place his cast, he somehow managed to embed the fly in my son's lower lip. Mercifully the other two anglers in our vehicle were doctors and were able to cut the barb off the hook and sterilise the wound. To cap a frustrating evening, I snapped the top section of my back-up rod trying to extricate a fly from the opposite bank.

Happily, after that pretty disastrous start, the level of pain evened out. The scenery was, as in the previous year, breathtaking; the sun shone more or less uninterruptedly, the water levels dropped further, we fished every minute of the twelve hours per day allotted to us, and we caught absolutely nothing. As did roughly forty per cent of the lodge.

It's a long way to go, and at no little expense, to fail. Paddy, though, was gracious enough to thank me fulsomely.

An interesting insight into expectations, it proved, too.

Lille: January 2017

The nature of a fishing memoir is that the vast majority of reminiscences come from those months between April and October, when one is actually to be found on a riverbank. In my case this largely matched the developments in my illness and the treatments. Thus, I was diagnosed in May 2013, operated on in that June, my first line of chemo started in August and so on ...

So, what are we doing here with an entry for January 2017 and the setting of Lille? There is of course a river in Lille, the Deûle, and it accounts for the historic strategic importance of the city, and the grandeur of the older streets there. But I'm not sure I'd want to eat anything that emerged from its waters.

When I reflect on the various phases of my illness, the one that often seems most rose-tinted is that covered by those sixteen or so months spent travelling to and from Lille. The rhythm was part of the appeal.

We'd rise at 5.30am and Jill would drive me to St Pancras to catch the 6.25 Eurostar. I'd arrive at approximately 9.30 (Continental time) and take the superb driverless Metro to the hospital. I would then cross the road and walk the seventy metres (we're on the Continent now so no 'yards') to the rather down-at-heel Hôpital Calmette, one part only of the sprawling CHRU. Such is the investment that the French have made in their health system that when I first started going there Loic and Arnaud felt compelled to apologise for its appearance; they have probably never visited Derriford Hospital in Plymouth. Then I would pay my hospitalisation costs and walk to the third floor to register before X-rays and an inspection, almost always from a junior doctor.

My schoolboy French was stale, unused other than to order drinks. No one other than Arnaud spoke English, so it had to improve rapidly. I now know how to discuss rather well in French some quite esoteric medical complaints.

And, once it was all over, I would go and find my favourite bar, the one by the attractive old Bourse, in which jazz music was always being played, to celebrate with a T'chi, a local beer, before returning to the Eurostar terminal.

In this whole place there were only two things that were unattractive. The first was the food, which was beyond unhealthy, and removed at a stroke any critique the French might offer of English cuisine. The second was the wait for the drugs to arrive from the pharmacy, which could take anywhere between three and five hours.

French hospitals do not offer patients Wi-Fi so to fill the dragging hours I would take with me photograph albums that needed updating. I had started putting old fashioned prints (remember them?) in leather-bound albums in the early 1980s and Jill had kept up with things until 2009, when the backlog started to build up. Even though it had become egregiously expensive in comparison with digitally assembled photobooks, we decided to keep going. So I would take over an album and prints and gradually we got up to date. I started with the pictures up to the close of 2012, and then did 2014 onwards. The year 2013 was still too painful to document, so I left that till last and finally managed to pluck up the courage in December 2016 to complete that one too.

But what then? Well, to fill the empty hours I did something eccentric even by my own standards. I took over my fishing diaries and inputted the data onto an Excel spreadsheet, and analysed the results.

I pride myself on a pretty laidback demeanour, so this level of obsessiveness (even if only prompted by the need to make time go more swiftly) took me aback, and properly.

If you're inclined to be bored by a discussion on flies perhaps you might like to skip to the next section ...

I started by looking at which flies had brought me most success on a salmon river (fewer numbers to count). The top ten, each fly expressed as a percentage of the total caught over the years, are set out in the table alongside. Many of the most knowledgeable anglers will scoff at such an analysis; salmon do not feed when they come back to spawn and attack with the only weapon readily available (their mouths) objects in the water that stimulate or irritate them. So the pattern of a fly is less important than the colour or size. The fly boxes of

FLY	%
Cascade	28
Tosh	16
Ally Shrimp	14
Munro	11
Red Monkey	9
Silver Stoat	6
Stoat's Tail	6
Red Frances	6
Blue Boy	1
Willie Gunn	1

two of the better fishermen I know contain respectively only Ally Shrimps or Stoat's Tails in varying sizes.

The reverse is true on a chalk stream, where trout and grayling will only show an interest in what they wish to eat. This means the fly life that is actually hatching (either from the riverbed and rising to the surface or floating on the water) at the particular moment you are stalking the fish. Hence the importance of 'reading the river' and 'matching the hatch'; these expressions may be ever-present, but critical nonetheless. And as the season progresses you see changes in the insect life; once the bonanza that habitually accompanies the two-week period of the mayfly hatch is over, there's little point fishing with such an imitation. Similarly, in the early part of the season you will see very few daddy long legs, but by September these large flies can be deadly. On the next page are my top ten trout flies.

TOP TEN TROUT FLIES	%
Gray Wulff	19
Pheasant Tail Nymph	12
Mayfly	10
Sedge	9
Hare's Ear	8
Daddy Long Legs	7
Klinkhammer	6
French Partridge	4
Alder (Flies & Beetles)	4
Iron Blue	3

The list itself leads one onto two areas of discussion. The first raged in the 1930s when the letters pages in *The Times* brimmed with views on whether it was acceptable to fish with imitation nymphs. This had been championed by the renowned angler G. E. M. Skues, who spotted that around ninety per cent of all fly life is taken by trout beneath the surface of the water, as nymphs hatch out of their eggs on the riverbed. The Pheasant Tail Nymph and the Hare's Ear (in total accounting for a fifth of all the fish I've caught on chalk streams over the years) fall into this category.

There is an adage that almost all flies purchased attract anglers not fish. I possess hundreds, possibly thousands, of flies in many different types of patterns. Yet over four fifths of all the fish I catch are on ten basic patterns. Food for thought ...

The meaning of loss: early June 2017

In June of 2017 was a day that began a week that will live with me forever, even though the recorded catch was a zero.

It was windy with plenty of cloud cover, the sun occasionally peeking through, and my guest was David Astor. We were fishing at Mottisfont on the Main beat.

The Test is an interesting case in land management. The river itself runs through a largely flat-floored valley and as a result can wander and meander, which over time it does, creating tributaries or 'carriers'. To protect the meadows abutting the various bits of flowing water, over the centuries landowners and tenants have managed banks, dug channels and on occasion altered the flow of the river itself. This has produced some interesting anomalies; for instance, on the Oakley beat at Mottisfont the banks are higher than the fields on either side. I had fished there for years before I even noticed it.

The Main, as the name suggests, is not a tributary but the principal part of the river. This changes the dynamics. It is about twice as broad as the other beats, in some places thirty to forty yards wide. It is also the only piece of water where we fish one bank and a different club the other. This doesn't really matter because, with a wood behind us for the entire stretch, it is impossible to cast to the opposite bank with a single-handed rod.

All rivers change shape and silt moves about, altering the lies of the fish from season to season, and sometimes from month to month. As a direct consequence of all of these factors, and belying its title perhaps, the Main has not been a happy hunting ground for club members in the past few years. So I arrived expecting a challenging day. This was exacerbated by the knowledge that the annual hatch of mayfly was abating and that by this point in the season the more aggressive of the fish had gorged themselves over the prior two or three weeks and might be sitting around rather as an uncle of mine used to do after Christmas lunch. The compensation for all of this was the companionship of an old friend and a lunch beside one of the Test's most appealing and eccentric lunch huts, overlooking swans, geese, ducks, dabchicks and coots as they landed on the stretch of water immediately below us.

As so often at that time of year, nothing really happened until the late afternoon, when the mayfly began to emerge from the water. By this time David had departed for some business meeting in London. At around six o'clock I was covering the deepest of the pools when I spied something coming to the surface, slowly and lazily slurping the flies down – usually an indicator of size. I stood back and observed. The next rise took place about a yard upstream, and some seconds later the subsequent one slightly further away from me. The trout was not staying in one position as they habitually do, but gently cruising along taking whatever came its way.

I cast, landing my fly a few feet above the previous take, only to see a gentle pool appear slightly further off from my bank. On the third of my casts the trout rose and took the fly. I lifted the rod tip and set the line and off we went. It was indeed a mighty specimen, immediately taking out fifteen or so yards of line, but with the tension on I got it back to within spitting distance of the bank. This continued three or four times with the fish going both upstream and downstream.

What was making everything even more exciting was that I was using a split cane rod, a twenty-first birthday present from my godfather. Once the most advanced technology available, split cane has long been overtaken, first by fibreglass and then by carbon fibre. These are much firmer in their action, generally making it easier to cast the line far and accurately. That said, the pliability of the more elderly rod means that when there is something on the end of the line, you feel it more. The sensation is just that bit more special.

And so it was with this mighty beast. The rod was bent into a shallow 'u', with the end twitching as the fish moved hither and thither. Truly these are moments of which we all dream.

But then the elements conspired against me. And how!

All healthy rivers have weeds. These are welcome – they encourage the insect life on which so much of the eco-structure depends. However, if they are allowed to continue growing a choking overabundance can be the outcome. So they are cut back once or twice a season. The first of these 'weed cuts' takes place in the middle of June, in other words a matter of a few days only hence.

There was indeed plenty of weed about, and I needed to keep the trout clear if I was to land it. I was managing well on this front when the line shot off downstream and, to my alarm, over the heads of a couple of swans. Majestic though these birds are, they are also petulant, very strong and not worth picking a fight with. So I let the quarry run a bit further to get the line past the pair, only to discover that I had been snookered. The fish swam under a clump of thick weed close to the river bottom. And there it stuck - with the rod bent heavily. I walked downstream with the tension tight and achieved nothing other than a few clicks of the reel. And so I crept upstream, past the swans, and then downstream again and so on. I figured that sooner or later the tension from differing angles would prise the fish out from behind the weed; but to no avail. Ten minutes passed, and then fifteen. And then ... well, nothing. The line suddenly went slack and I had been defeated.

On the way back up to London in the car I ruminated

about my day, as I always do. At first my mind turned around the frustration of it all. What if those swans hadn't paddled ever so elegantly between the weed and the bank? What could I have done differently? Had I been at fault? But then I reflected that if this sport was that easy, wouldn't it be called 'catching'? And hadn't I had the privilege of tussling with a fine adversary for about twenty minutes.

Each morning after a day on the river I write up my fishing diary. Here's what I entered the following morning:

'The curse of the Main? Well not really. Lost the fish of the season (5lb+) when it got stuck between two swans and some weed. Embedded itself there for 15 minutes before the line broke. I thought grrrr, but on reflection drew contentment.'

Immediately after writing those words I went to the Marsden to see Sanjay Popat. We were reviewing the results of my latest scan. Calmly, and as ever humanely, he advised that this had revealed that my tumour had grown; not hugely but enough to presage that my days in Lille were likely to be coming to an end. The immunotherapy treatment would soon be over.

These are devastating moments. You are never sure what will come next, if indeed there is anything. And, in my case, if there were to be no 'new big thing' then the writing would truly be on the wall. The horizon always comes much closer in until one knows.

But the next seven days brought an event that set my own private worries against the context of a national disaster. In the early hours of 14 June, the fire at Grenfell Tower took place. The final death toll from this ghastly tragedy was seventy-two, of whom five were current or former students of an adjacent secondary school with which I am closely connected, the Kensington Aldridge Academy.

How small my travails seemed now ...

Respite of sorts: late June 2017

My involvement with the Kensington Aldridge Academy (KAA) had begun just over two years previously. I remember walking along the Thames near Tower Bridge when Lucy Morris, a friend and trenchant supporter of Blue Sky, called and said the academy was looking for a new Chair of Governors; I must apply. I pointed out immediately that I knew next to nothing about education, my own had not exactly been a shining example and anyway I had a terminal illness. As I did so, I opined that each one of that trio should surely rule me out completely.

I repeated these reservations both to the head-hunters and then to the interviewing panel, so it was more than a surprise when I was offered the role in July 2015.

The academy itself was a brand-new school, built on a piece of hitherto underused land in North Kensington abutting the arches of the Hammersmith and City Underground line. Until the millennium, the borough of Kensington and Chelsea had had insufficient secondary school places for the children of its residents. Much to its credit, it had in a little over two decades developed two academies, of which KAA was the second, with the potential to educate approaching three thousand eleven to eighteen year olds. Our academy had opened in September 2014 with a single year group; by the time of the fire it had grown to approximately eight hundred students.

All corporate bodies seem to have disaster recovery plans these days, and I'm sure KAA had one of sorts. Quite possibly an excellent one – but wholly inadequate to address what stood before us on the morning of 14 June. Lucy and I made our way around midday to the offices of Adam Balon, our fellow governor. These were located about three hundred yards from the tower, which was still aflame. I had spoken already a couple of times to John Brown, another governor[24], who was desperately concerned for the whereabouts of a family friend who had been living in the tower. He had given me a taste of the wholesale nature of the tragedy

---

24 The board of governors of KAA was extremely highly qualified, another factor making me doubt my own appropriateness as chair. They included Sir Merrick Cockell (former Chairman of the Local Government Association), Sir Rod Aldridge (founder of Capita), Adam Balon (co-founder of Innocent Drinks) and John Brown (former owner of *Viz* magazine). At the time of our Ofsted inspection some months later, another highly successful member of the board opined: 'I never quite understood why a school like this had such a stellar board. But then the tragedy happened and it made sense'.

unfolding, as well as the scale of what to expect.

Adam had immediately given David Benson, our principal, and his leadership team the use of his offices. There were about ten teachers there, wearing what they had hurriedly put on at two, three or four o'clock in the morning. So T-shirts, jeans and trainers. They were all hollow-eyed, and making activity the bulwark against worry and sadness. Sixty or so of our students had lived in that building; at this stage we knew some were missing, although we had no idea of how many. But anyone looking at the smoking hulk could only fear the worst. What was immediately clear was that we were very unlikely to be granted access to the school anytime soon. KAA lay yards only from the base of the tower.

It was a measure of David and his team that there was already a plan. And a good one. One of the largely untold stories of Grenfell is the cohesive power of the community. And in our case that meant especially the local educational network. The principals of another local academy, Burlington Danes, and a private school, Latymer Upper, had each called offering whatever help was needed and, critically, free space. By midday the plan was coming together and senior staff members had already made the necessary visits. The deals were done.

That afternoon I convened an emergency board meeting with a threefold aim. The first was to ensure that David and his team could move forward quickly in the knowledge that the board had sanctioned the plan; secondly, to establish an emergency sub-group with delegated authorities to enable us to adapt to what was inevitably a fast-moving and harrowing situation; and, finally, to demonstrate to the outside world that it was business as usual to the extent that was possible. As it turned out the board's rapid response was to prove essential. As the scale of the school's dislocation became apparent, extensive new and additional funding was clearly needed. In our direct negotiations with the Department for Education we were able to provide a rapid turnaround in budget preparations and approvals and also to instil confidence in our ability to manage them. Of course the bulk of the credit lies with David Benson and his team, but the governors really went above and beyond anything that might have been expected of them in the days immediately after the fire, and indeed in the months to come.

A further achievement of that day was to set the tone of KAA's communications to the outside world. This was captured in our press release and read: 'Like other parts of this tight community, Kensington Aldridge Academy has been deeply affected by the tragic fire at Grenfell Tower. Our first thoughts are, as you will understand, for those students and members of our staff who live in the building. We will do everything in our power to help and comfort students, members of staff and local residents. Our school is located only a few yards from the fire, and has, we are afraid, suffered as a result. At this point we do not know when we will be allowed back in to assess the damage. In these circumstances it was impossible for us to open today, and we do not anticipate being able to open on a fully operational basis in our current premises on Silchester Road for a while yet. As soon as we know when this might be possible we will share this with all our students, their families and our staff'.

This was crafted by David and me that afternoon, and agreed by a wider but still very small group. In our shocked state, we really just uttered what we felt, and in parts the message was contrary to some of the advice of the PR specialists helping us. But unwittingly, perhaps, the line was the right one. It emphasised the pain the community was going through, it said where our focus was (students, families and community) and it underlined our independence. As the whole debacle became politicised and as the anger set in we found ourselves unaffiliated with the many agencies in the firing line for actual or perceived inadequacies.

On Friday 16 June, two short days afterwards, David led a series of assemblies for each year group in the school. Lasting an hour apiece, they were as cathartic as they were moving. I attended them all, as indeed did the whole governing body, not one of whom that I can recall retained a dry eye throughout the morning.

Thus began a pretty intense period for me personally. My role at this time centred on the administrative, the anticipation of problems and very occasionally the management of emotions among key players. Notwithstanding my original forebodings about my unsuitability for the role of an academy chair, with the benefit of hindsight it became apparent that it was a good thing that the school had one who had little else to do (other than occasionally to go fishing). As the subsequent year was to prove, I had signed up for what became around three days a week of hard and sometimes draining work. And here again my illness provided a silver lining; all those consultations on the subject of my terminal condition had rendered me pretty steady in the many occasionally stress-ridden and emotional meetings that ensued.

Happily, and as respite, I did still manage to escape to the riverbank from time to time that June and July. Two days that really stuck in my mind were 24 and 25 June, a Saturday and Sunday.

The early part of the Saturday I spent at the Speech Day at Wycombe Abbey School. Jill was absent but I still had an enjoyable time watching Daisy play her saxophone (surprising her father into the bargain) and compete in the odd athletic event. Even here though, and in spite of it being a weekend, Grenfell intruded. I took several calls from our volunteer PR adviser who had received a series of calls from *The Sunday Times* on some article they were researching. His job was simple: to keep us out of the press at all costs and, on this occasion as on others, the plan worked.

My invitation to fish was only for the Sunday, but I arrived in Stockbridge on Saturday evening in time for an early dinner with my host, Ashe Windham, and his guest, both of whom had been in the same boarding house as me at school, forty years earlier.

The Houghton Club, of which Ashe is a member, is

arguably the most prestigious fishing club there is. Limited to around twenty-five individuals, it owns several miles (on both banks) of the Test, as well as the Grosvenor Hotel on the High Street in Stockbridge, where I was staying; there in the club room, reserved for members, I joined them both. It has some wonderfully arcane rules. All fish landed must be taken out (killed), presumably so that no member has to face the indignity of hooking something previously caught by someone else. Either breakfast or dinner must be taken off the river in the club room thereby enabling members to see each other occasionally and the day's catch is limited to eight.

I hadn't expected to fish that night. However, with dusk falling and the day just about over, Ashe invited me to tag along, rod in hand, and encouraged me to cast at anything that might rise.

It was a calm evening with sufficient light that even at 9.30pm you could see rises here and there. So, as the other two disappeared, I wandered upriver, crossed a bridge and at the first pool espied a fish gently taking something on the surface of the water. With my first two casts I negotiated myself into the right spot and on the third my fly was gently pulled under. I struck and soon realised that I was in for some sport. It was not just that it was plainly taking out plenty of line, it was the aggression and speed with which it did so that alerted me to the likelihood of a rainbow trout. The indigenous brownie can grow to a prodigious size but, pound for pound, a rainbow will always fight harder. With the light falling I played the fish, counting my lucky stars that the pool was wide with no overhanging branches and, it being late June, there was little or no weed.

Within ten minutes, by which time it was close to pitch dark, I had wrestled the trophy to the bank.

The seeds of the miraculous:
October 2017

As with the adjective 'iconic', so too is 'miraculous' vastly overused. And in the process it risks being cheapened.

However, when you have been told to your face several times in the space of a few months that you are 'a medical miracle', as has happened to me, you are forced to ponder a little. The more so, if one of those offering the opinion is a member of your medical team.

Looking at the beginnings of the process that led to this pronouncement, the inevitable impression is the reverse of anything dramatic. As is so often the case, a sequence of events that might be described as momentous has its roots in the mundane.

In my case it was two telephone calls, both taken on the riverbank.

Autumn 2017 saw the final of my fortnightly

pilgrimages to Lille. I was feeling more than a little bereft, and though plainly in fine physical shape and a picture of energy I was in fact in the grip of dull anxiety. The horizon that is my life expectancy had come in again, and I perceived it to be at around the twelve to fifteen-month mark. That is, in the absence of anything unconventional turning up.

That pair at the core of my revered medical team, Loic and Sanjay, were searching around for something new. There were a number of ideas and a short, if bafflingly titled, list of potential drugs. The first step, however, was the testing of my genome.[25] Two years on and the rationale for this is clear, though I'm not sure it was to me at the time. I just trusted my doctors.

It was on the River Dun in late September 2017 that I took the first of these calls - the initial corner piece of a new jigsaw. The day was a glorious example of the Indian summer we were enjoying that year. The sun was shining through the trees at the bottom half of the beat there as it makes its way between the National Trust woods on one side and the sleepy Romsey–Salisbury railway line on the other. This is the favoured part of my favourite place at Mottisfont. My reverie was made all the more intense because, as so often happens in September as the heat of July and August diminishes, fish life tends to become more active in advance of the coming winter.

---

25 A genome is defined as the complete set of genetic information in an organism. It provides all of the information the organism requires to function.

It was early afternoon and I had about three to four hours of activity ahead of me. My mobile is always switched on, though if I'm honest frequently on mute; as my professional life has become less frantic, most mornings I never receive any calls at all, and I often forget to switch on the ringer from the night before. This particular day we were in luck though, and the ring tone was so loud it might have been audible to those in any passing train. A transatlantic call – even more out of the ordinary. It was from someone at Carys, a medical analytics company. Courteously I was asked to hassle the insurers to authorise the expenditure on their service so that they could request a sample of my cancer cells. And that was it, three or four minutes of what had become a routine occurrence these days. Other than being mildly irritated at having my labours interrupted, I didn't even give it another thought. Until much later ...

The most stubborn diseases are frequently sourced to or created by mutations in our DNA. In my case, the relatively light dosages of asbestos to which I was exposed at work in the eighties would not have led to mesothelioma in the vast majority of instances had I not had the genetic makeup that provided a fertile bed in which it could develop. But just as mutations are a curse, they can also be a lifeline. If you can attack them with a specialist drug or, in the parlance of the medical sector, a 'targeted therapy', then you might be able to bring down the whole pack of cards. With me this would be temporary only – but respite is respite.

If I appear to write knowledgeably, I mislead. As in

previous points in my recent life I had no real understanding of the science at that point. The extent to which I grasp it now has only come about with the passage of time. My more simplistic view of what we were about was this. There was a potential drug trial in Leicester that represented my next best hope. The drug was called Rucaparib. The trial was due to open at any time and the man orchestrating it was Professor Dean Fennell. A significant proportion of my fellow sufferers have a genetic mutation known as BAP1. The testing of my genome should demonstrate this and, if we could get me enrolled, off we'd go.

The second seemingly unremarkable telephone call I took on 6 October. The weather was again fine, truly reflecting Keats' 'season of mists and mellow fruitfulness'. My companions were Graham Wood and Celina Francklin, who had been in the manner of a penfriend when we were both undergoing chemo exactly four years earlier, she for breast cancer. Her husband, William, had been a frequent partner in crime at Eton and has been a sound friend of mine over five decades.

Just before lunch I took a call from an 0116 number – not one I recognised. The panel on my mobile told me it came from Leicester, and in fact it was from the University College Hospital there. On the line was one of the nurses in Dean Fennell's team. Would I be free to come and see him the following week? Another appointment with another doctor – since 2013 there had been certainly plenty of those.

So I barely gave it another thought other than to

comment to my two companions as we sat down to lunch that I sensed the beginning of a new chapter.

Our meal was followed by quite an afternoon. In October, the action can often be sluggish and slow as the season winds down. I was at the bottom of the beat close to where it runs down into Kimbridge. There is a pool there of some depth and apparent tranquillity which can hold a number of fish that have grown fat and strong during the course of the summer. But none of them appeared interested in the offerings I placed before them, from a juicy Daddy Long Legs on the surface (frequently a potent weapon) to a weighted Creeping Caddis far below – and everything in between. Fingering my way through my fly-boxes, I came across an item I had never previously used and whose provenance was a mystery – a large white fluffy nymph.

I tied it on and was completely unprepared for what happened next. There was a swirl of activity and a lunge for the fly. Within a couple of moments it was evident that I had lured up from the bottom one of the kings of the river. A few seconds later it had set off downstream taking twenty-five to thirty yards of line. I tightened up the tension on my reel, only to savour the fact that it appeared to make little or no difference.

Some minutes before arriving at the pool, I had just lit a Monte Cristo No. 4 – my habitual post-prandial treat on the river. In my youth I had smoked cigarettes, around a packet of Gitanes a day. The craving to smoke had always been most acute when outdoors. When my mother, who routinely got through fifty cigarettes a day, died of lung cancer in 1991 and I was clearing out the family home I discovered a stash of around one hundred and fifty packets. In my anger I burnt them all ceremoniously throwing the remaining few I had on the pyre. I have never had a cigarette since. But I needed something akin to the deep gravel you find on the side of steep hills to save out-of-control lorries. For me this came in the form of Havana cigars. And these days there is the added excitement of watching the reaction of some of my more puritanical friends at the sight of a lung cancer sufferer lighting up a stogie.

So there I was, with a strong fish some way below me firmly on the hook and a cigar between my teeth. And thus it continued as I wrestled away, moving slowly downstream over some duckboards across a stretch of bank given over to reeds. I eventually netted the mighty warrior by climbing off the duckboards and wading through to clear water, in the process soaking my trousers and footwear – but I wasn't letting a minor hitch like that deny me. And how long had this battle taken me? My only guide was that there were only two or three puffs remaining on my Monte Cristo. An eccentric but strangely apt way to measure the passage of time.

The postscript to this part of the story is this. At the time of writing I have yet to take a single dose of Rucaparib, but Dean Fennell was to play a decisive role in what was to become a one-man drugs trial.

Going home: July 2018

Throughout the second half of 2017 and the first half of 2018, the Kensington Aldridge Academy had continued to occupy a very significant amount of my time, particularly during the school's term time.

The initial post-fire challenge had been to find physical premises from which to operate. The deal with our generous hosts (Burlington Danes and Latymer) finished at the end of the 2017 summer term, and by that July it had become transparent that we would be unable to reoccupy our own building.

So it was on a brown field site on the edge of Wormwood Scrubs that we relocated to a purpose-built temporary facility constructed by Portakabin. How it came to be built in two months was beyond me – I believe it holds the record for being Britain's most rapidly constructed school of recent times.

Once we had moved into the new quarters, rapidly

christened KAA2, our collective focus became the forthcoming Ofsted inspection. Though these things are random and therefore unscheduled, the existing rules mandated that a new school must be assessed before the end of its third year; for KAA this meant by July 2017. At the time of Grenfell we were still awaiting an inspection, though in the weeks immediately thereafter it was plainly inconceivable that we would have been subjected to one. The longer the autumn term continued, the greater the inevitability. When it came, in early December, it turned out to be a rigorous but ultimately successful affair. We were ranked 'outstanding' in all categories.

The great unknown for the school in the early months of 2018 was how long we would remain in our Portakabins. Whilst in many ways our new home was adequate, there were very good reasons to want to go home. First, KAA2 was the best part of a mile from our original building, which created a logistical challenge for pupils and parents. Secondly, and maybe as a result, discipline was suffering and as we discovered when the exceptionally fine summer weather broke upon us, concentration too. In short, there was a groundswell in favour of a return as soon as practicable, the best date being clearly at the start of the next school year, September 2018. Throughout, the relevant government ministries (Housing & Local Government and Education) were at pains to emphasise that there was no pressure on the school, though of course the more thoughtful civil servants believed that having us back was going to be a positive step for the local community.

There were three significant obstacles. Were the staff and student body in favour of the move and could they face the inevitable proximity to the scene of the disaster? Ditto the parents? And, finally, would the board of governors be able to vote in favour of it?

Not one of these was straightforward. David Benson was at pains to ensure that any vote on the issue had to be overwhelming, both amongst pupils and parents.

The position of the governors was also complicated. The first rule of any governor is to ensure the safety of teachers and students at all times. And this posed a range of questions for us as a board. Was the tower safe in its current state? How could we ensure that it continued to be safe? What happened if its condition deteriorated such that it became a threat? And what was the legal position of the governors if a further tragedy were to happen as and when the tower was taken down?

We all started to discuss it in earnest around the February 2018 half term. That left oodles of time, we thought, for a decision in May/June.

The board quickly endorsed the staff plan of acclimatising the students with taster visits back to the original school. I meantime, with help from others, began to think about a board decision, which we broke into three areas. Was the building at that point in time safe to reoccupy? How could we future proof that position? And how could we be assured that, even if our students were in no physical danger, we would not be harming their mental wellbeing?

With experts advising on mental welfare and building safety issues (both plainly beyond the professional ambit of any governor) my focus narrowed to getting the board into a position that would enable it to vote for a return. And straight away we hit a massive snag. The legal advice was clear: if further disaster did occur, those who took the decision to move the school back, the governing body, would have to bear responsibility. At its most extreme, that might even extend to corporate manslaughter. School governors are all unpaid volunteers, and such a potential liability, however remote and hypothetical, seemed out of all proportion to what could be expected of my colleagues.

At an early meeting with Nick Hurd[26] (the designated government minister and well-suited to this role) I asked if it were possible for governors to benefit from an indemnity. Upon consultation, of course, the answer was no; governments cannot exempt individuals from what might become criminal charges. The problem thus remained.

By the end of June the decision making had been hit by many delays, including the difficulty of procuring a definitive independent survey on the safety of the Tower. I remember one meeting at that time with

---

26 Nick Hurd and I had seen a lot of each other when he was Shadow Charities minister in 2007-10, and then afterwards when he was a minister at the Cabinet Office. His constituency was situated less than two miles from Blue Sky's offices. He was an early and strong advocate of Blue Sky and always a good person with whom to bat ideas around.

representatives from two ministries and the local authority (over twenty civil servants in all!). Halfway through for some reason I came to the conclusion that we should ask the Government to mothball KAA2 for us just in case the stability of the tower did deteriorate; in this way we would have an 'escape route' readily available. If the Government agreed, the forthcoming governors' decision would then be of a different and much lower order of magnitude, precisely because (in extremis) it could be reversed.

I wrote my thoughts on a piece of paper and shared it with two or three of the KAA team; each responded that the cost would be prohibitive and therefore the request was bound to be refused. Well, there was no point in not asking.

So I raised it in a subsequent telephone call with Nick Hurd. I explained the sheer magnitude of the challenge for governors, and he promised to raise my proposal with the Cabinet ministers responsible.[27] Within a few days it was clear that, notwithstanding the expense, we would get something along these lines, expressed within a letter of comfort.

This arrived in the nick of time for the governors' meeting on 3 July, the final point at which we could have voted in favour of the move before the start of the autumn term. Never before had I prepared so rigorously for a single meeting, closeted for hours with our lawyers.

---

27 Respectively James Brokenshire at the Ministry of Housing, Communities and Local Government, and Damian Hinds at the Department for Education.

My father had always opined that 'time spent in reconnaissance is rarely wasted'.[28] Excellent advice, as it turned out, for it was an arduous meeting lasting three hours but, as ever, the board of governors rose to the occasion.

We were heading home.

28 Dad had obviously read his Sun Tzu.

At sea: August 2018

There are a number of places that have made a deep
impression on me that do not feature in this book.
That, I'm afraid, is the inevitable consequence of
pursuing the theme I have chosen. So only passing
mention is made of skiing, and of Salcombe, that
beautiful town in South Devon that only appears en
passant at the start of this tale.

The house built by Jill's parents (John and Betty
Langham) sits alone at Scoble Point with a commanding
view on three sides over the estuary. It has been the site
of adventures and joy aplenty as the children grew up.
When the bulk of them were in their teens we would
decamp there for a fortnight in August each year with,
on occasions, up to a dozen of their friends. There Jill
and I worked like navvies, cooking meals, clearing
rubbish and messing about in boats. Each night we'd
retire to bed, physically and mentally exhausted, but

more often than not enraptured by family life.

There have been times in my life when I have found myself at Scoble entertaining doubts or fears about the future. This is not the fault of the house or its setting – rather the opposite; its very seclusion and the other-worldly pace of life there gives one plentiful opportunity to contemplate. So it was on my frequent visits in the early years of the new millennium, when I had real worries about what to do with my working life. And so it was when I went down in early August 2018.

My treatment was at something of a crossroads. My third line of chemo had run its course[29], though Loic, comme toujours, was upbeat. My medical team had now been augmented formally by another genius, Professor Dean Fennell. Two months previously he had told us of this genetic mutation present in the cell tissue from my tumour; it was called the PTCH1 or 'hedgehog' gene. It is either incredibly rare or non-existent (such is the paucity of data nobody really knows) in mesothelioma, though relatively common in the skin cancer known as advanced basal cell carcinoma. And the good news about that was that there was a clinically approved drug on the market, Vismodegib. I remember writing it down in my notebook.

But a more or less informal conversation in June had not become an established route by August. I had not seen Dean since the news of my relapse and to make

---

29 This came in the form of the pill Vinorelbine; it had done its job in holding the tumour in place for six months but the July scan had shown that things were on the move again.

matters worse a consultation in Leicester had been cancelled at forty-eight hours' notice, an event I found truly destabilising and caused by 'NHS resourcing issues'. I was planning to make the trip from Devon to Leicester three or four days hence in the hope of establishing Vismodegib as his preferred option, and then getting Sanjay (who as my oncologist would actually prescribe it) and Loic onside. Even then, there was no guarantee that this would end up being my treatment – the manufacturer (Roche) might not release the drug and, even if that could be achieved, who would pay? My supposition was that the insurers would never cough up and so it would have to be a raid on my already dwindling pension.

Thus I arrived in Devon, hung over to boot following the very agreeable wedding of a very glamorous goddaughter of mine in Norfolk. I walked straight into a lunch where the guests included Mark and Amanda Sater, longtime family friends who, like us, are part-time residents of the town. They have children broadly the same age as ours, and whole chunks of summer holidays over the years have been spent together. When Mark suggested spending the afternoon mackerel fishing I leapt at the chance.

The fly purists tend to wrinkle up their noses at mackerel. When you hit a run of them anyone can catch them, often with many on the same line simultaneously. And what do you do with dozens of mackerel – a strong-tasting meal at the best of times?

I have some sympathy with this view. Sea fishing is a different type of sport. My diaries reveal some astonishing catches, including a three-hundred-and-forty-five-pound blue marlin caught off Bora Bora in 1990, nine sailfish in a single morning off Kenya in 2010[30], yellowfin tuna, wahoo, kingfish and so on. The excitement of these still resonates, but looking into my inner soul I would have to admit that in each case I was little more than a happy winch. The boat's skipper on these occasions was the reason for any success.

But all this should not take anything away from the sheer fun of deciding on a whim to go off and catch some mackerel, hangover or not. To do so, we had to leave the estuary and head out into the open sea. And what a day for it! The sea was almost glassy in its smoothness, and the sky a deep cerulean. Mark had certainly acquired knowledge since our largely fruitless trips of a decade or more earlier. We headed about a mile offshore and drifted inwards on the tide. Hard work it certainly wasn't. I puffed away on a Monte Cristo whilst sipping lager from a can. Every so often we checked our rods, and more often than not there would be one or two on the lines. Most we returned but the larger ones we dispatched for the pot. Two hours later we returned with the sun beginning to dip. We had landed between twenty and thirty, but kept only a handful and the following day we ate the resultant pâté.

In its own way, a perfect afternoon and evening and as on many other occasions the brow had unwrinkled as my troubles receded.

---

30 Then a resort record and one which still stands, I'm told.

'Celebrate tonight, come on':
29 September 2018

The twenty-ninth of September 2018 was a day I had long anticipated. It was my sixtieth birthday and, since my diagnosis, a fervently held personal target. Originally I had given this milestone only a minimal chance of being attained, on making it through surgery I had marked it up to forty per cent, and as time went by I came to see that it might very well happen.

Jill and I had talked long and hard in the fifteen months prior about how to celebrate it. Though our thirtieth wedding anniversary also fell in the same month, we decided to make a splash of my birthday. A celebration of my survival, too. Early on Jill pulled off a masterstroke, typically, by booking Brooks's Club, of which I had been a member since 1997. With the date falling on a Saturday, when the club is officially closed, we were able to have the run of the whole building; this was fortunate as I had completely lost control of the numbers invited. I had thought that not many people would want to come to a birthday party in London at the weekend. As it turned out, we were juggling an acceptance rate greater than four fifths. I had been advised the maximum for a sit-down dinner was one hundred and twenty; that evening we were at one hundred and sixty.

Maybe because it was our party, or maybe not, we felt there was a real buzz in the air that night. Brooks's may have some very stuffy members, but it has an exceptional staff, and much of the subsequent exuberance was certainly due to them. One and all they appeared to love a fiesta. And so, apparently, did our guests.

Just before the end of the dinner Jill made a speech which was as moving as it was warm and witty. At various points many guests were left in tears by the elegance of her words and the humour they contained. By now you should have a fairly accurate read on me, but Jill offered up some angles you might not have seen. For example, her summary of me went like this:

'Fundamentally he's just an old hippie – never happier than when at home wafting around in one of his extensive collection of Kenyan kikoys, listening to music, drinking a martini or smoking a cigar (hopefully outside) and surrounded by his children. He is a proud and loving father but hopelessly disengaged when it comes to any detail of their education or activities. I have sometimes, to my mind unfairly, been accused of being a "helicopter mum" but the children much more accurately refer to Mick as "space station Dad", so remote is his orbit. By way of example, at a school lacrosse match not so long ago he introduced himself to someone he thought was another parent, only to find she had been Honor's housemistress for the previous three years.

'Aside from his family, the overwhelming love of his life is fishing – trout, salmon, grayling, mackerel, wahoo, sailfish, marlin – really anything that swims or flaps. His tally this year is fifty-seven already and this is mapped with uncharacteristic and forensic attention to detail after each trip on an Excel spreadsheet which slices and dices the data – chronicling daily average catch, by beat, time of day, month, and fishing companion. He is never happier than when setting off with the dog and a picnic and boxes and boxes of identical-looking flies for yet another day of dangling his rod in a pretty tributary of the Test. It illustrates his love of the countryside, his unexpected ability to focus single-mindedly for hours at a time, his fondness for hunter-gathering and his happiness in being solitary.'

The following day I opened my presents. Whenever I'm asked by Jill beforehand what I might want for Christmas or a birthday, I always say the same thing: 'A million quid and a new lung'. I had literally no idea what I might be given on this occasion, and really wanted nothing (except perhaps the new lung).

Over drinks I was handed an envelope containing a voucher entitling me and one other to spend a week fishing at the fabled Estancia Maria Behety on the Rio Grande in Tierra del Fuego. Half an hour earlier, Richard and Susu Elliott had unexpectedly arrived delivering a card. All now slotted into place. Jill had recruited him as my nanny.

Plenty to stay healthy for, then.

Hope springs eternal: 17 October 2018

This was the final day of the fishing year for me and one for which, to be honest, I held out very little hope of success. As we drove to the river, I was trying to manage the expectations of my guest, Mark Sater. There were clouds overhead and a steady, if not heavy, rain was keeping the windscreen wipers busy. On our arrival, Graham Wood was on hand and greeted us with optimism, reporting having seen a steady alder fly hatch in progress. He felt sure we would have fun.

As I put on my waterproof I was in no way convinced, but I still took from him half a dozen imitation alders. We were on the Dun at Dunbridge, which splits into two environments. Above the bridge opposite the lunch spot it is broadly open and faster flowing; below it the water moves more slowly and has some deep and shady spots, where the overhanging branches on the opposite bank are a natural trap for the misplaced cast.

Fish were steadily rising down there and I set to work. Within ninety minutes, when we broke for lunch, I had netted three and had probably lost the same number. There was something plainly going on. Were the trout bulking up for the impending winter?

Mark and Graham came back with news of a huge grayling - over two pounds - and a quick and happy lunch ensued before we reported back for duty.

Four hours later and at 5.30pm it was time to pack up. The light was closing in and the rises were tapering off fast. In the afternoon I had landed a few more, and lost probably as many. Mark, meanwhile, had caught another sizeable grayling and a small wild trout. This was an extraordinary conclusion to the angling year for me. Hitting your daily limit is absolutely not what might be anticipated mid-way through October and in the rain.

How does one assess quality versus quantity? Mark and I fell into a discussion on the drive back about our contrasting days. Whilst I had filled my boots, he had achieved something far more remarkable in my view. The second grayling he had caught had also topped the two-pound mark. With their high golden-edged dorsal fins, grayling are to my eye the most attractive inhabitants of English rivers, and wholly wild. Just as it is rare to catch a wild brownie of over two pounds, so it is with grayling. Two in a day was quite something, and I honestly maintain to this day that I would have traded my haul for Mark's. He was unconvinced but finally came round once I had established (via Google on my mobile) that the largest grayling ever caught in England weighed four pounds four ounces, and the sixth largest two and three quarter pounds.[31]

The high spirits of the day had deflected my standard thought patterns at the end of each season since my diagnosis – namely, will this be my last full one? I am a far from morose individual, but you will understand that this has become a natural reaction since 2013. I find myself reflecting on joyful passages recently ended and wonder if I will see their like again. It's the same at the end of each skiing season. This sense of time passing was exacerbated by the knowledge that the options for treatment were shrinking.

Since the start of September, I had been taking my daily Vismodegib pill. In so doing I had been advised that I was the first mesothelioma sufferer world-wide to be treated thus, quite possibly the first within the much wider cohort of lung cancer patients. Truly I represented a one-man trial. And because I was the only data point, no one could predict what would happen.

A week after this magical day on the Dun, Jill and I found ourselves in the waiting room of the clinic at the Marsden. I hoped I was hiding my extreme anxiety, but I doubted it. The specialists there hot-desk, and over time we have met Sanjay in three or four different consulting rooms. My worst fears seemed to have been confirmed when we were shown into the one in which

---

31 The largest was caught on the River Frome; the sixth biggest two miles downstream from where we had been fishing.

he had told us in January 2016 that my remission was at an end.

'Oh bugger', I said. 'My unlucky room!'

'No Mick,' he retorted, 'your very, very, very lucky room'.

In two months my tumours had shrunk in size by over one third.

Girl power

On 7 October 1922, Georgina Ballantine hauled in the largest salmon ever caught on a British river; the river was the Tay, and the fish weighed sixty-four pounds. This has very little to do with my tale, except that it is a powerful parable with which to illustrate girl power.

Though not popularised as a concept until the arrival of the Spice Girls in the 1990s, girl power has been a reality that has been with me my entire life. I grew up in a family with a sister either side of me and my mother ruling the roost when my father was at work. This reality continued as my own family evolved, with four daughters to a mother of strong temperament. The boys and I are, I believe, admirably self-sufficient, but the odds are not always with us.

Many people have asked me about the impact of my illness on domestic life. In all probability, that impact fell most directly on the girls. At the time the storm broke upon us in the early summer of 2013, Paddy was travelling and Ivo was in the first year of life at Bristol University (which, if I remember such times accurately, will have been something of a haze).

India-Rose, then aged seventeen, was there early on when we shared that memorable June day on the Dun. She was taking exams, her AS-Levels, and the intensity of the revision undoubtedly transported her to a more arduous but protected place. She and Honor came to visit me in my room at the Cromwell once. I was sitting in a chair and they both jumped onto the bed and immediately started playing with the remote controlling its height and angle, in peals of laughter as they sought the most extreme position available. Honor would appear to have inherited my sense of humour and, though the younger, was a raucous ringleader in the action. It came as light relief to us all – so much better a harmless diversion than false humour and awkward questions, the answers to which would more than likely have been evasive ... or just as awkward.

Lara, our eldest, was also slap bang in the middle of exams – her university finals – when the diagnosis emerged. She knew, of course, of talk of tests and hospitals, but we tried to shield her. I have no doubt that we failed, but the exams themselves took her focus elsewhere, and that brought comfort to Jill and me. Upon my release from hospital, the very first outing we made was to attend her graduation. I remember well the drive to and from Cambridge, surrounded by cushions in the front seat of the car to ease the aches and pains. I recall also my pride as Lara collected her degree, looking far too young and pretty to have achieved such eminence.

At the time I think we worried most about what it was doing to our youngest, Daisy. The others were all closer in age, and sufficiently mature, we hoped, to be able to take on board what was happening. But Daisy was only ten years old. To make matters worse she was the only one who was based at home continuously in 2013. In late summer, we were discussing with Loic another family with a father afflicted by the disease, whose youngest child was only twelve at the time of his diagnosis. Jill spluttered that Daisy was only ten, to which our redoubtable surgeon responded: 'Oh, but I'll be coming with you both to her wedding'. I think he still believes it, bless him.

Our children tried to cover it up, of course, but every so often the hurt and confusion came through; occasionally a seemingly harmless joke at someone's expense would touch a raw nerve. There were a couple of those, certainly. And I think realisation dawned at different times for each of them. India-Rose confided recently that in those initial summer months she was sufficiently anaesthetised with shock that she was just determined to get on with things. However, four months later, in her words, she 'stupidly Googled the prognosis of mesothelioma' and it was only then that pain replaced numbness.

Throughout all of this Jill somehow managed to keep the show on the road: charming to all, but battling on my behalf with hospitals and medical staff, where necessary.

Her notebook was always at the ready to take down conditions, potential side effects and remedies, all of which were wholly unfamiliar to us. How many miles on my road to semi-health do I owe to her?

The effort of protecting me and the family must have been overwhelming, especially for a person whose reflexive action is always to try to make everything just right. The nature of the weight she was bearing became evident in the run-up to that first Christmas. I was in the latter stages of my first line of chemotherapy, and I can only imagine how exhausting I must have been to live with, and she was trying, in spite of everything, to ensure that this was the best one ever. I found her one night reviewing her plans for the children's stockings, weeping inconsolably. And there was nothing I could do that would help.

But good can often come out of pain and distress. India-Rose, in her characteristic way, said she was 'grateful' (her word) that it shook her into never taking the family for granted. Lara expanded on this, and I repeat her words in closing, verbatim.

'So much has changed, and we have learned so much along the way, but the fundamentals of how our family operates remain the same. If anything, the experience of Dad's illness has made us closer as a family; fiercely protective of every one of us; each acutely aware of others' moods and concerns. Maybe every family feels that way, but to me what we have is special ... and in some twisted, convoluted way, it is due in part to the cancer.'

Don't cry for me:
Argentina, 13–18 January 2019

Four months after that vibrant and unforgettable sixtieth birthday celebration, Richard Elliott and I departed for Argentina. I had never been to Latin America before, and frankly had never expected to go there. But what a treat in store.

Perusing atlases at home had in no way prepared us for what we were about to experience: the journey from Buenos Aires to Ushuaia appeared quite short but actually took three hours in a jet. And the contrast on landing was dramatic. BA, the 'Paris of Latin America', was balmy in temperature and sophisticated in style, whereas Ushuaia, which boasts the most southerly commercial airport in the world, looked exactly like what it was – a frontier town, with fierce winds whipping down the Beagle Channel.

It was a two-and-a-half-hour drive from there to the

estancia, the first forty-five minutes of which were spent going over the end of the Andes. This also took me by surprise, as I thought the Andes ran north-south. This is indeed the case for the vast majority of their length, but when they reach Tierra del Fuego they turn abruptly left and travel the last hundred miles or so eastwards, ending up at the Atlantic Ocean.

To the first-time visitor, the flatlands north of the Andes offer a beguiling landscape. Look to the south or west and the snow-capped mountains lie on the horizon, overlooking the pampas. The terrain is not wholly flat with gradual rises and falls. The odd escarpment appears to have been formed by glacial movement aeons ago, with seemingly flat plateaux on their summits. For me it was redolent of a Western film set, maybe in New Mexico.

Overhead the occasional condor might be spotted, and on the ground guanacos, close relatives of the llama, are freely seen. No longer hunted, they are curious of humans and can gather to watch in herds of thirty or more. Beavers are pretty common too. Otherwise the estancia is the home to cattle, horses and thousands upon thousands of sheep, and boasts the largest shearing shed anywhere on Earth. Livestock are herded by traditional gauchos, another powerful reminder of a bygone age.

So, a place rich in atmosphere – and that's before we get to the fishing, the reason we had travelled the vast distances to get there. The Rio Grande meanders through this expansive landscape and as it twists and turns it offers pools of varying shapes and sizes. This flatters the fisherman in one important respect. The winds there increase in strength during the late morning, daily reaching speeds in excess of forty miles per hour, and sometimes above fifty. It is impossible to cast into them, but with the wind at your back within a few hours you sense that you are beginning to handle your rod like a pro.

We were fishing for sea trout, or more accurately 'sea-run' brown trout. In the 1930s a certain John Goodall had imported the humble brown trout, as legend has it, from Loch Leven in Scotland. Instead of staying put, as might have been expected, they had promptly made a break for the sea, where food supplies were substantially richer and more abundant. These creatures multiplied exponentially in size, sometimes topping twenty pounds and fairly routinely fifteen, before returning to breed in the Rio Grande.

What greatly enriched the experience for us both was the quality of the guides. Allocated one to a pair of anglers each day, we got to meet them all, and they were all highly knowledgeable, with good English. Some were more gregarious than others and, like all country people, it was a pleasure to spend time with them.

And they could be very funny. On our first day we fished with Genaro, renowned for being something of a bull-shitter. The subsequent day was with his cousin, Frederico, who observed: 'You can always tell when Genaro is lying, because his lips move'.

We settled into our groove pretty quickly, though, the

truth be told, the finer points of catching sea-run browns were new to us. For example, when a salmon takes a fly you let a little line go out before lifting the rod and setting the hook. I had caught a couple before I learned that with these you had to strike on contact. But that appeared not to be holding the two of us back. By the end of the first day we had both enjoyed good fortune, Richard catching one in the 'witching hour' as the sun was setting around 10pm that weighed in at sixteen pounds. Everything was recorded, of course, but there was a book at the lodge which recorded only those fish of fifteen pounds or heavier. It was an added mark of pride to catch one that would 'go into the book'.

By an irony, Richard and I were at our most effective in the first half of the week whilst we were still working out what was going on, with our potency peaking on day three of our stay when we landed ten between us. Strangely, after that, the better we seemed to be mastering the arts, the harder the sport became. Angling is often like that though, isn't it? I think our early success was more down to the lottery that is the allocation of the pools rather than anything else. Certainly a couple of the other guests had fairly quiet openings to the week, and with at least one of them we had to endure a very long face for the first couple of dinners. Richard and I celebrated almost as hard as that eccentric Frenchman when he finally caught his first fish. We were less enthused when his turn duly came for the more fecund pools, and at supper each night he regaled us with tales of his prowess, exclaiming 'incredible' in a Gallic accent every few sentences.

However, the slight tailing off in our hit-rate mattered not a jot. We continued to catch one or two each day, and that was really the key to what was a consummate time. Unlike some of my other trips over the decades, I would get up in the morning pretty much knowing for certain that during the day I would catch something, and more often than not something mighty. The prospect of a lengthy journey for a blank week is the stuff of nightmares for fishermen; the opposite is therefore a golden-edged dream. And in Tierra de Fuego that rapture was edged in greater gilt for being situated in so sublime a setting and with such delightful people.

As we boarded the flight back to Gatwick I vowed to myself never to return. I feared, quite probably irrationally, that a repeat would struggle to match up and thereby mar the memory of the original visit.

Up the Varzuga: 11–17 May 2019

I consider myself blessed to have avoided the blues, at least since the end of the annus horribilis that was 2013. There's been plenty of anxiety from time to time, but I have been fortunate in being seldom if ever down for more than an hour or so. But on arrival back from Argentina that is exactly what happened.

And this was all the more surprising as we were in the middle of the finest conditions in the Alps for a generation, with plenty of skiing planned. But, after occupying myself for a couple of days in writing up our adventures, cataloguing photos and cleaning and sorting equipment, I found myself wholly out of sorts. A sure cause of this was the amount of time I had on my hands, now that the school kept me busy around half a day per week only (as opposed to the three or so immediately post-Grenfell). And it was probably the case that the side-effects of the Vismodegib were beginning to take their toll. First, I had lost my taste buds to something called dysgeusia – a well-established side effect of the drug; although a small price to pay, it robbed me nevertheless of the enjoyment of most foods and drinks. Secondly, it had become the norm for me to be woken up a minimum of twice a night with spasms in my feet, calf or thigh muscles, not only causing me physical pain, but denying me sleep as well.

However, over and above these factors were the conflicting emotions of elation at the whole Tierra del Fuego chapter, and the dread that my illness might cheat me of future opportunities to catch more large sea-run fish. I just couldn't bear that thought.

Strangely Jill had been prescient in anticipating this: when I broached my desire to go off in pursuit of another adventure in 2019, she was remarkably understanding. And thus, in a few short weeks, I found myself set to head off to the Varzuga River – considered by some one of the world's best for salmon – in the Russian Kola Peninsula.

I tried to persuade a couple of my friends to join me, but to no avail – they were busy. So I went alone. When I booked, I was concerned lest I find myself spending the week with the over-competitive, or the boring, or the plain obnoxious. It has been an axiom of mine that I have never met an unsympathetic angler, but in truth it's not quite the case: in my time there have been a couple who tried my patience in the course of a single lunch. So I sought what I termed a 'no-tosser guarantee' from Charlie at Roxton's, the booking agent.

In the helicopter down to the river from Murmansk, I surveyed my fellow travellers. There were seven of us in all. As I was to learn, the core of the group was medical – dentists, orthopaedic surgeons or medical entrepreneurs. The majority had fished before at the Lower Varzuga camp, and tossers they proved themselves very definitely *not* to be. They were welcoming of me, even to the point of enquiring as to what I did in life and, somehow, I'm not quite sure how we got onto it, the state of my health. A keen rivalry did develop between the two highest scorers, but it was maintained with charm and no needle. When we gathered at lunch or dinner, polite enquiries were made as to how things had gone, and the success of others was the cause of celebration. And, boy, did we laugh. There was any number of jokes, plenty of a schoolboy hue. And, by a process of evolution, increasingly they ended up with the punchline 'Up the Varzuga'.

My stay in Russia was also enhanced considerably by the presence of Yegor, my Russian guide. I had been warned that in comparison to Argentina they would be useless. Certainly there was a skills gap, as well as a language barrier – Yegor had only limited English – but, as with rustic people the world over, he had a dignified straightforwardness and gentle warmth. As a result of the limited number of guests I had him to myself, so I spent more time in his company. We chatted about football, the more productive ways of fishing employed by the locals once we had all departed, and his recovery from a vodka addiction. Masses really – but never politics. He smoked way too much and his eyesight was going – we lost at least one fish at the net because he could not see it. And he really should have gone to see a doctor about his waterworks, needing to relieve himself three or four times every hour. On several occasions I called for him to bring a net as I had a salmon on the line only to be greeted with the plaintive cry: 'Sorry, Mick. Busy. Piss'. We became firm friends in a very short while.

We arrived on Saturday 11 May. Two days later, 13 May, I found myself standing in water flowing past my waist. Yegor was on the lookout for icebergs, capable of bowling us over – and painfully, as I had already discovered – even though they were growing increasingly small as the thaw continued. Facing south-east that morning with the sun streaming into my face and bouncing off the water, I felt something approaching rapture. How was it that, six years to the day from that fateful visit to Medic, I was here still? Embracing life and in great health. It was the only day of this week that I failed to hook anything, but it was the one worthy of the greatest celebration.

At this point, I had caught only one salmon, and was steeling myself for another thin trip. I asked myself, as I managed my cramps that night, what abject failure would look like. Less than five fish felt like real disappointment; on the other hand over thirty – then a seemingly unattainable target with only four days left – looked like outrageous success. Anything in between would feel like gradations.

I need not have worried, as it turned out. The following morning, a horridly wet one, on the pool beneath where we usually ate lunch, I caught four in the first ninety minutes, the same in the next hour and a half, and eleven in total by the time we got into the boat at 12.45pm. As the morning progressed, Yegor's radio was crackling unceasingly and he jabbered away excitedly. When we arrived at lunch everyone seemed to have heard about it. Getting out of his boat one of our group embraced me saying: 'We knew it was you, Mick. Our guide didn't know your name. But we were told that the man doing all the catching was "the one who's always happy"'.

Such a compliment, for that is how I saw it, moved me greatly. Who wouldn't have been happy?

As it turned out, better was still to come; providence saved up its finest for the week's conclusion. By breakfast on the Friday I had caught thirty-three salmon and I was licking my lips at the prospect of the coming day. The morning was to be spent at the bottom-most pool on the river, known as 'the Beach'. As we motored down in the boat, two fish eagles were arcing overhead – a great omen, I remember thinking. And thus it proved. Earlier in the week I had fished this pool from the boat, but with the river levels dropping we were now able to do so on foot. Almost immediately we found evidence that the salmon were running, and in numbers, as I caught my first within ten minutes. Indeed I think that morning I met with success just about every fifteen minutes, for within the first hour Yegor had netted four, and another three in the subsequent one. 'Come have a cup of tea, Mick,' I remember him pleading. Under normal circumstances a break might have been welcome, but how rare is it to find oneself in exactly the right place at exactly the right time? So I denied him his well-earned cuppa, instead preferring to keep our noses firmly to that metaphorical grindstone. And it paid off. By 12.40pm, when I was virtually dragged into the boat by Yegor, the score was twelve. Twelve!

I'm not sure what I was expecting the afternoon to be like. Surely I had used up all of my favours? That was certainly my thinking as we made the short ride across the river to the pool opposite the camp itself.

Known as 'the Larder', it was deep with a fast flow just a few metres from the bank, and had to be fished very much on terra firma. Slip off the bank and your life jacket would have saved you, but not before you'd been whooshed half a mile or so downstream.

I was proved wrong on one thing though; my good luck did hold firm, though tempered a bit. The weather even obliged; with the afternoon sun shining brightly and steadily, I found myself hooking a salmon more or less every half hour, rhythmically almost, ending the session with a further six in total.

So, eighteen in a day. I have caught bigger fish than I caught that Friday, but never more.

In the helicopter back to Murmansk the following day I found I had an abundance to savour. Fishing at its best has many, many components, of which the catching is an important element. But if it were the only element then it might not be the passion it is for me. And as I ruminated I concluded that, happily, that week I had derived every bit as much pleasure from the company of my new friends as from the ridiculous haul I had to record in my fishing book.

An advance in the treatment of difficult cancers: Professor Sanjay Popat

Over the years, Jill has proven herself to be one of Cancer Research's most effective fundraisers. This started in 2012, and has continued with added urgency since. In November 2019 she arranged a dinner at the Bank of England, the charitable focus of which was Cancer Research. To this end she asked Sanjay to write a piece. Other than quotations, his are the only words in this book not written by me, and I include them for two reasons. First, an objective view of my progress seems to complement my subjective one rather well. Secondly, and more importantly, there are aspects of my case that are clearly ground-breaking; what they are and where they point are better set out by his authoritative words.

'Mick is a remarkable individual: an absolute

testament to the cutting edge of modern cancer research.

'By all predictions, Mick shouldn't be here. He has a terminal disease: a diagnosis of malignant pleural mesothelioma – a lethal and devastatingly progressive cancer of the lining of the lung, through no fault of his own. But last year (2018) he celebrated his fifth anniversary, and he continues to thrive. His story is not one of chance and good fortune, but is the story of the resolute determination of cancer scientists, cancer researchers, and oncology trialists, pushing back the boundaries of cancer medicine through the tenacity and application of modern cancer research: research of the type funded by Cancer Research UK.

'Mick has received treatments all evaluated and developed by scientific research: major complex surgery, the anti-angiogenic drug Bevacizumab, Nivolumab immunotherapy, and most recently precision oncology through genomic sequencing. His oncologists, Professor Dean Fennell and I, identified a simple but novel mutation in Mick's cancer – a change that meant his tumour was driven by an abnormally active molecular wiring-pathway called 'hedgehog'. We started Mick on Vismodegib, a highly effective but simple daily tablet that switches off hedgehog wiring – his cancer shrank down beautifully and, importantly, he has stayed in remission for over a year.

'This magnitude of benefit is unheard of in mesothelioma but is not a miracle. It is, in fact, the application of years of scientific research to the clinic.

That's the point of cancer research: to make a difference. Science and cancer research are the reasons Mick is here and is doing so well.'

A pause to the saga

The end of this tale has been clear from the second chapter, if not the first. As I have been heard to comment, I know everything that is going to feature on my death certificate except the date.

But to close on such a note would be quite wrong. For starters, I have never been one for sad endings. And those not already bored by my ramblings would, I feel sure, find themselves tiring were they to endure even more tales, either from the river or the consulting room.

Finally, this feels like the perfect point at which to pause. It is, after all, a moment of real optimism and therefore ideal for looking back and reflecting on events. I currently find myself, as Sanjay Popat puts it quite unequivocally, 'in remission'. My cancer has shrunk and has undergone a complete metabolic response to the drug. Put more simply, it has gone to sleep – it is completely inactive. And how blessed am I, for this is 'unheard of in mesothelioma'. Normally patients have tests to find out what has gone wrong; by contrast, I am now being subjected to probes attempting to find out what has gone *right*. And this may not be a moment of real hope for just me alone; if I am not that uncommon in my genetic mutation, oncologists will have a potent new weapon with widespread potential to aid fellow sufferers.

All this taken into account, though, we have to be realistic. The tumour is still there and will sooner or we hope later wake up and get all aggressive again; that, I'm afraid, is the nature of my burden. And at that point the merry-go-round of consultations leading to an agreed next route will begin once more. Then, of course, at some point (much further down the road, we pray) we will run out of options with which to biff the cancer, and not that long thereafter that will be it for me.

From the first word I wrote, I knew that the whole premise of this book was offbeat; and the way in which it was compiled was unorthodox too. I picked episodes of my recent life, more or less at random, and as I tapped away on my computer where all of this might be going was something about which I was most uncertain. However, as the words piled up themes began to emerge and take on significance, even if only in my mind.

'What a long strange trip it's been', sang that great sixties band, the Grateful Dead, from their incomparable hit Truckin'. And were I to condense the past seven years into seven words, then that line seems spot on. If I had believed the statistics at the outset of my cancer diagnosis, I had what the industry describes as long months or maybe short years in prospect only. But it has turned out otherwise, and very much so. Sure, I may have very little hair remaining and I'm the victim of nightly cramps, but in every other respect I lead a completely normal life.

At an early stage you might remember that I was determined to put five times as much living into my remaining days to compensate for what I was going to miss out on. This has always been accompanied by my abhorrence of the concept of the bucket list. However, there is an implicit conflict between these two positions. Without the itemisation that such a list would provide, how can I gauge my progress at shoehorning in all of that additional living?

Quite evidently, one (of a number of) silver lining(s) of my early retirement was that I have been afforded the opportunity to spend more time on the river. Noodling about with the piscatorial data that I had originally consigned to an Excel spreadsheet in Lille, I found an answer by proxy. It turns out that comparing the period from May 2013 to today, with that of the start of my fishing records to that month, I have enjoyed on average four times as many days on the river since my diagnosis. And it would appear that my performance has improved too, with the average number of fish caught annually rising by a factor of around eight. As Gary Player so eloquently put it: 'The more I practise the better I get'.

So this beloved pastime has provided me not just with a multitude of days spent by a river, it has also assured me, albeit through an eccentric mode of

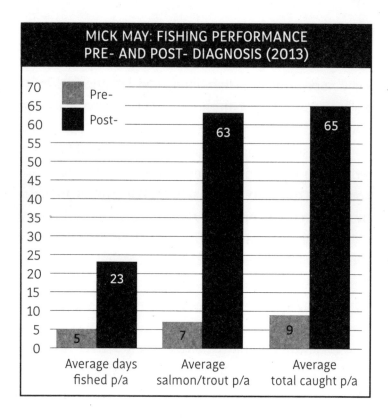

comparison, satisfaction that I really am making good on my pledge.

These scribblings may, I hope, be light in style, but it would be wrong to make the assumption that I have not been pondering about life's rich tapestry. The past seven years have given me plenty of opportunity to consider the meaning of it all. I'm no philosopher and I would not ever claim to have discovered anything profound for mankind as a whole. But I have been able to work out some fundamentals that matter desperately to me.

I have habitually found New Year's Eve more worthy of melancholy than celebration. Most often, the outgoing year has been one in which I have found contentment and had fun, and the incoming one offers only hope. This reflects a characteristic on my part to look back and audit the immediate past. In my mind, therefore, is a catalogue of my favourite years. So it might be something of a surprise to say that if I were to draw up a list of my top ten, it would almost certainly include 2014, 2015, 2016, 2017, 2018 and 2019. I am very much the happy man that the Russian guides saw.

How on earth can that be?

Much of it is down to good fortune, and what I term 'ending well'.

The way in which my professional life came to an end was as good as I might have wished. That it did so was due rather more to my colleagues than to me I feel sure – probably entirely, actually. However, I feel in the minority in celebrating a blessed conclusion to a career; I have observed that many of my contemporaries find the act of winding down their working lives to be a time of personal challenge. Rare is the friend who proudly declares 'I'm retired and happy'. And I might well have been in the same boat had I not had to make hard decisions following the onset of my illness.

More centrally still, I wonder how many people take their families for granted? Before 2013 I would have protested strongly that I did no such thing. I was then a caring if forgetful father, and loved them all very dearly. But I had never stopped to wonder what each child and Jill meant to me. And, being truthful I might have let the odd niggle here and there remain unresolved. Having the horizons of life drawn in and tightly defined led me to readdress any untied emotional shoelaces that there might have been. And as I did so, and as time went by, I came to the simple conclusion that there was nothing, bar nothing, that I cared for more than my family.

Like Dorothy in *The Wizard of Oz* I know that in spite of all my adventures there is no place like home.

If that is the case, and very surely it is, why write a book called *Cancer and Pisces* - one about fishing and living with a very nasty disease?

Sweet as my life is, I find it hard to record the broad sweep of an illness against the domesticity of home life. What I have tried to portray here, though, is how time spent on the river wove itself into the tale of my illness and vice versa. Over the past seven years one has provided something of a golden thread to the story of the other. And at the same time there is a rather beautiful contrast between the deep dull dread one feels immediately before receiving the results of a scan and the bright anticipation of packing my tackle into the back of the car before driving to the Test.

And the vivid shaft of light that fishing has offered has been a natural and vital element in my joie de vivre. At my lowest points I could always look back happily to a sun-dappled evening in Hampshire, or forward to some future challenge.

As, indeed, I am doing right now ...

Acknowledgements

This book is, in truth, a love-letter to Jill, Lara, Ivo, Paddy, India-Rose, Honor and Daisy. Their support for me demands a gratitude for which mere words seem insufficient. My lasting appreciation is due also to my wider family, alphabetically surnamed the Hoveys, Langhams and Scarratts.

Nor can pen and ink do justice to my debt to my medical team. Simon Moore, Brian O'Connor, Loic Lang-Lazdunski, Sanjay Popat, Arnaud Scherpereel and Dean Fennell (in the chronological order in which I met them) are not only sources of wisdom and inspiration, they are also amongst the most humane and decent people I have ever encountered.

In similar vein I owe a very great deal to Ian Bailey and Jo Jefferies, who personify integrity (and ensured that none of our meetings was ever dull).

As my recent life has evolved St. George's, Campden

Hill has played a central and spiritual role. It and Fathers James, Peter and Neil and the Reverend Dana have a special place in my heart.

Many kind and good people have asked me to fish with them over the years. I would like to say here how grateful I am to them. That they do not all feature in this book is no reflection on the pleasure I took from our time together – rather that one feature or another of my illness did not intrude on the day(s) we spent together. The list includes Charles Booth-Clibborn, Roger Lambert, Toby Stubbs, Bob Campbell, James Straker, Jules Smith, Harry and Claire Fitzalan-Howard, David and Cissy Walker, the Packard family, Chris Pease, Patrick Lees-Millais, Simon Woolton, Nick Downshire and James Johnstone. One or two of these I envy greatly as they are, to use an apt description of a wise ghillie, 'able to catch a fish in a puddle'.

A number of friends have been generous in reading the manuscript of 'Cancer and Pisces' in earlier incarnations. They are Markie Peel, John Brown, Lucy Morris, Carwyn Gravell, Dougie Rae, Graham Wood and Susu Elliott. There are three people to whom I owe special gratitude in this regard, namely Barney White-Spunner, Philip Dunne and his daughter Evie.

If you see a really, really great photograph in this book it will have been taken by Hugo Burnand who enthusiastically offered all that he has taken of the family over the years. I am much in debt to him, not only for this, but for a great many other kindnesses to us all.

More than a mere thank you is owed to Jonathan Aitken. It was he of course who suggested this project and took my initial pooh-poohing graciously. His encouragement at various points has been critical, not least when he pushed me to seek a recognised publisher, rather than to print a few copies privately. It is true to say that without him, 'Cancer and Pisces' would never have happened.

Which brings me to Quiller. The draft that emerged from the copy editing process is, in my view, vastly superior to the one that entered it. For this the credit must go to my editor Sue Bassett. And without Andrew and Gilly Johnston you would not be reading these words. It has always been an ambition of mine to write a book; however, I never anticipated that it might appear in any bookshop, for the simple reason that I could not believe anyone might find my musings of any interest whatsoever. I hope fervently in this regard that I am proved very wrong and Andrew and Gilly are proved very right.

Mick May
June 2020

CANCER
RESEARCH
UK

O nce upon a time it would have been nigh on impossible to conceive of a happy and fulfilled life following the diagnosis of a terminal illness. Those days were probably only a few years, possibly a couple of decades, ago.

Mick's story is testament, however, to that fact that it is now a reality. This is so because of huge advances in medical treatment. Some of the drugs from which he has benefited were only in test tubes at the start of his tale. This in turn speaks powerfully to the impact of research on our lives.

In gratitude he has asked that any money he might receive from the sales of this book be gifted directly to Cancer Research UK. CRUK is the largest independent funder of research into cancer in the Western world, and is responsible for developing and paying for over 50% of all research into the disease in the UK. Almost its entire budget for this comes from private donations and grants.

Mick would urge any reader who would like to help support the charity's heroic work to visit the website (www.cancerresearchuk.org); for those wishing to follow his example and make a donation of whatever size they may do so by arranging payment to: -

National Westminster Bank Plc,
PO Box 221, Connaught House,
65 Aldwych,
London, WC2B 4EJ

Bank Account: Cancer Research UK – Regional Receipts

Account no: 22994270

Sort Code: 56-00-13

IBAN: GB79 NWBK 56001322994270

BIC/SWIFT: NWBK GB 2L

CRUK, Quiller Publishing and Mick would like to thank you in advance for any donations made.

R. Brora

Glen Cannich

Delagyle, R. Spey
R. Findhorn

Conaglen

R. Whiteadder
Rutherford, R. Tweed

R. North Tyne

R. Laggan, Islay

R. Ure

Loch Corrib

R. Shannon

R. Maigue

R. Usk · R. Coln

R. Kennet

R. Wylye · R. Itchen

Mottisfont, R. Test

Rawlsbury Lakes

Salcombe

Locations as featured in Mick May's fishing diaries
~ Britain and Ireland